Slow Train to Auschwitz *Revised Edition*
Memoirs of a life in war and peace

Peter Kraus

Slow Train to Auschwitz (revised edition)
Print: 978-1-76109-719-5
Ebook: 978-1-76109-720-1
Copyright © Peter Kraus 2026
Cover design by Graham Davidson
First published 2026 by
GINNINDERRA PRESS
PO Box 2 Bentleigh 3204
ginninderrapress.com.au

Preface to Second Edition

I was originally motivated to write my memoirs to leave a record of my side of the family for my children, grandchildren and their descendants. It was with some surprise to me that when the book was published it drew comments from people as to the importance of recording my family's holocaust experiences. Since that time I have become associated with organisations such as Courage to Care and the Queensland Holocaust Museum and Education Centre and come to realise more fully just how important a preservation and dissemination of this history is.

I was aware as I originally wrote my memoirs of deficiencies in my knowledge which left holes in the narrative, in particular I knew next to nothing of the rest of my family's experiences. Since then I have had some valuable information about the train journey from Mr Miki Granski, Dr Balog's grandson. In addition my cousin Sylvia Deutsch OAM has come across her late father's, my father's brother's, memoirs. Sylvia kindly photocopied these for me. Apart from being both fascinating and delightful reading in its own right it has provided valuable information about the experiences of my paternal family living in Slovakia. This complemented information I got earlier from my cousin Dr Jasz (formerly Elfer) Istvan in Budapest, known in the family as Pisti, about the maternal side of my family who endured their war in that city.

My sincere thanks to Debbie Lee, now my publisher, for her help and encouragement in updating this record.

Peter Kraus
January 2026

Contents

Prologue	7

Part One - From European Roots to New Australians

Escape from the Camp	15
Karoly Krausz and His Descendants	17
Fulop Krausz and His Descendants	21
The Elfers and Partoses	22
Imre and Klari	24
From Subotica to Austria	26
Life in the Camp	30
Other family during the war years	36
Life in Postwar Europe	38
Budapest	42
Back to 1946 or 1947	43
Emigration: The trip to Sydney	46
Other Family	51
Work and Life in Australia	54

Part Two - My Story

Schooldays	62
Hobbies	71
My First Car	76
Camp Bevington	78
University	81
In the Real World	87
Back to University and the Teaching Hospitals	90
Hospital Residency, Launceston	95
Marriage	103
Albury, Part 1	107
Crown Street	114
England	120

Oxford	124
Work at Swindon	125
The Consultants	127
The Registrar	129
Looking To Move On	133
Harlow	136
Europe	140
The Short Course and the MRCOG Exam	143
Bad Decisions	145
Albury Part 2	148
Wodonga	149
Horses and Cattle	152
Wodonga Specialist Practice	154
The Hawkesbury	156
The Good	160
Rotary	161
Flying	163
The RAAF	171
The Bad	178
Disaster	182
Goodbye Windsor	183
Townsville	186
Kirwan Hospital to the Townsville Hospital	191
Bribie Island, Locums and Retirement	194

Part 3 - My Spiritual Journey

Before We Start	205
My Origins	206
My Journey	209
God's Chosen People?	212
Jewish or Christian, or Can You Be Both?	214

Peter's memoirs deserve a wide audience. They not only capture one family's story, but encapsulate the upheavals of twentieth century Europe and the story of Australian migration. As a child survivor Peter is a witness to the Holocaust, as a migrant he shows how Australia provided opportunities for its newcomers to flourish, and through his life journey he finds his identity. His family owes him a debt of gratitude for recording our own history, and also for sharing his experiences for posterity more broadly. Such a testament becomes part of the historical record.

Sylvia Deutsch OAM, (Peter's cousin)

Prologue

When I was a university student in the early 1960s I worked in my free time in a couple of camera stores. One particular incident is etched in my memory.

I assisted a lady, of the same generation as my parents hence a little older than I, who wanted to buy a camera. I asked her the usual questions as to the type of photography she wanted to use it for, what her photographic experience was and her price range.

Based on her answers, I told her she had a choice of two cameras: the Kodak Retinette 1a, or a small Hanimex camera. I explained that the Hanimex was slightly better value for the same money as it had a few extra features and, although not quite as well finished as the Kodak, was nevertheless quite reliable. There was not really much to pick between the two, so it boiled down to personal preference.

She looked at the Hanimex and asked where it was made. I told her Japan. She asked where the Kodak was made and I told her Germany. She pointed to the German-made Kodak, said she would have that, then she shook her head sadly and looking at me said, 'You're too young to remember.'

I did not tell her where I had come from, as I did not want to lose the sale and leave the poor lady without a camera.

She was referring of course to the atrocities perpetrated by the Japanese during the Second World War with which Australians were only too familiar, the war in the Pacific having come right to our doorstep, indeed over it. Most people are familiar with the bombing of Darwin but the Torres Strait Islands also got a good pasting and I believe a bomb was even dropped on Sydney. Three Japanese midget submarines penetrated Sydney Harbour, inflicting some damage before they were destroyed. A composite midget submarine consisting of recovered parts of two of them can be seen at the Australian War Memorial in Canberra.

Bombing and submarine attacks, horrible though they may be, are nevertheless part of normal warfare. What the lady buying the camera was referring to were Japanese atrocities witnessed by Australian troops in the Pacific theatre, particularly Papua New Guinea, and also to the Japanese treatment of prisoners of war, many of them Australian.

Fortunately, the world moves on and Germany has for a long time been a respected and valued member of Western civilisation and is a leading light in the European Union. Nevertheless, when my wife and I visited Austria and the concentration camp at Mauthausen in the year 2000, there was still an almost palpable feeling of guilt among the Austrians, including many of the young adults we met who can hardly be held responsible for the actions of some of their grandparents' generation.

As for the Japanese, I was a member of the RAAF Specialist Reserve for twenty-eight years and was at one time on deployment in Timor Leste (East Timor) as part of the Australian contingent of the UN forces performing a peacekeeping role there.

The Timorese culture puts a lot of value on debts owed and their repayment. The Timorese felt that Australia owed them for the help given to Australian forces during the war, often at considerable cost of horrible reprisals by the Japanese. They felt that the part played by Australia around 2001–2, at first on its own and later as part of the UN forces, had cancelled the debt owed them by Australia.

Forces from different UN member countries played different roles during that peacekeeping period. The Japanese were assigned a civil engineering role, rebuilding roads, bridges and other such infrastructure. This was carried out by Japanese soldiers of an engineering regiment. So well did these young Japanese carry out their task, and in such good spirit, that the Timorese felt that they had cancelled out the considerable debt their grandfathers had incurred by their behaviour a half century earlier.

World War I, initially known as the Great War, was hoped to be the 'war to end all wars'. Despite this, many feel that the seeds of World War II were sown in the first war and especially in the terms of the Versailles Treaty of 1919 that ended the war.

World War II was, I believe, one of the most significant events in all human history. Unlike World War I, there was great justification for it. A madman racist white supremacist megalomaniac called Adolf Hitler had risen to power in Germany and decided to conquer the world and rid it of undesirable forms of the human race, including Jews, gypsies, homosexuals and others. That sounds like the unlikely plot of a superhero movie but it is all too true. Apart from war casualties, six million Jews and ten million Christians who didn't agree, together with many others, were deliberately exterminated.

World War II was what stopped him and not only won the freedoms we enjoy today but began to shape the world into that in which we now live.

War accelerates technological progress like nothing else. World War Two's technological advances ushered in the jet age that has revolutionised travel, the atomic age with both its benefits and risks, advances in radar, anaesthesia, blood transfusion, antibiotics and much more. Dr Wernher von Braun's V2 rocket, the first intercontinental ballistic missile, was the embryo of the space age.

Working for a time as a volunteer at an aviation and war plane museum, I discovered to my distress that today's generation has very little idea at all of this important event, even apparently well publicised parts of it such as the Battle of Britain. And yet this war, so significant in shaping the world as we know it today, is very recent history indeed.

Today's generation are significant in that they are the last to have any direct contact with people who were actually there. I was born in the middle of that war and have only a few muddled childhood memories and am now in my late seventies. My parents were much more closely involved of course, and my grandchildren did know their great-grandmother before her passing. They also know my aunt (actually my mother's cousin) Susan. Now in her mid nineties, she is the last of her generation in our family and was a young adult during the war and endured the same as the rest of my family.

They say history repeats itself and it is only by knowing what has happened in the recent past that we can try and prevent that. Is it not ironic that while we say 'Lest we forget' and genuinely appreciative crowds line the routes of marches on Anzac Day, there are so-called 'Holocaust deniers', and others among us who try to rewrite history for the sake of political correctness?

With regard to pre-war Germany of the 1930s, it is as well to realise two things. The first is that we are unwilling to accept truths that are not palatable and this is what enables the most horrendous things to happen. Stories of racially motivated atrocities in 1930s Germany filtered through to the rest of the world but they were so horrible that people just did not want to believe them. After all, the Germans were the most civilised nation in Europe, maybe the world; such things could not really be happening there, surely?

The second thing is that the ordinary German was just an ordinary man or woman who happened to be born in that country. None of us can choose where or who we are born. Thus the average German soldier in Hitler's army was just a citizen doing his bit for his country like his English, American or Australian counterpart.

Regrettably, there is a racist, bullying element in every society and that includes ours. What happened in Germany in the 1930s was that political circumstances allowed a charismatic leader such as Hitler to gain power and those elements in society were given the opportunity to throw their weight around, and everyone, having become accustomed by gradually increasing exposure to acceptance of their beha- viour, followed the crowd.

This must be a warning to us to be vigilant and not allow the wrong things and the wrong people to gain power, as a modern version could easily happen in our society today. And yet it is happening. Under the guise of increased tolerance, our society is losing freedom of thought, freedom of speech, freedom of conscience and freedom of religion. Unfortunately, this is very much the case; it is not alarmist or exaggerated to acknowledge it.

I have lived through much of this change in our, and I refer particularly to Australian, culture. My parents, brother and I, the first of our extended family, migrated to Australia in 1948 when I was six years old and I went to school here from 1949 to 1959. I remember our teacher in 1951 explaining proudly how Australia, now so multicultural, was then '95% British stock'. All my childhood storybook heroes, such as Biggles, were British. My brother Paul's first book, titled *The Not So Fabulous Fifties*, was subtitled 'When bread was white and cheese was Kraft'.

We arrived at the end of 1948, just as 1949 was about to usher in the huge wave of European migration that so altered this country and shaped it into what we take for granted today. The large influx of Italian migration especially had a huge impact. Can you imagine a country where no one had heard of veal, Italian food was a can of Heinz spaghetti and a cappuccino was unknown, although Nescafé was the go? No pizza. You could eat Chinese, although it was a bit of an adventure.

This then is the story of one family group in one aspect of that war, and one member of that group in particular, who somehow survived and, coming to this country to make a new life for themselves, tried to leave behind the horrors they had experienced and with their contribution helped shape Australia into what it is today.

Part One
From European Roots to New Australians

Escape from the Camp

In April 1945, thirty-one-year-old Krausz Klari (Clara Kraus) borrowed a pair of pliers from the bootmaker at the Nazi slave labour camp between the village of Viehofen and the town of St Polten in Austria, a little west of Vienna and not too far from the concentration camp at Mauthausen. At that time, she did not know that her husband Imre was an inmate of Mauthausen.

They had lived in the formerly Hungarian town of Szabadka, which had become the Yugoslavian town of Subotica when Europe was carved up by the 1919 Treaty of Versailles following the armistice which ended World War I. With the rise of Hitler, the Nazis press-ganged Imre and other Jewish men into forced labour.

Clara, in early pregnancy, her two-year-old son Peter (me) and other Jews were evicted from their homes in Szabadka/Subotica and interned in a ghetto, from where they were sent by train, packed like sardines into cattle trucks with no facilities, to concentration camps such as Auschwitz for extermination.

When Imre and the other men in the forced labour gang were starved and exhausted to the point that they could work no more, they were sent to Mauthausen to be exterminated. At least 90,000 people perished in Mauthausen and its satellite camps, Imre's brother-in-law, Clara's older brother Andor (Andrew) being one of them. He died of typhus the day before the camp was liberated.

All too many of those who were in Mauthausen at its liberation by the 11th Armoured Division of the US 3rd Army on 5 May 1945 died as they were so ill and malnourished at the time of liberation. This despite the Americans setting up field hospitals to do what they could for the survivors who needed this care. Imre was one such, he being so ill at the time of the liberation that he had lapsed into unconsciousness. His friend carried him to the Americans, who nursed him back to some semblance of health. The liberation was only just in time to save him.

Clara at the time knew nothing of this. What she did know was that a man by the name of Losleben, a kindly old guard at the labour camp, had warned her to escape. As the Allies advanced through Europe, the Nazis evacuated such camps before the Allied liberators got there. This was not only an attempt to hide the atrocities from the Allies but also fulfilled their aim of killing as many Jews as possible while they still could.

Clara used the pliers to cut the wire fence. Escaping was not difficult but until then it had been safer to stay in the camp than to wander around the countryside. So Clara, her son Peter (me), her baby boy Paul, who had been born in the camp in October 1944, together with her uncle, Jeno Partos, his wife Elizabeth (née Frankl) and their twenty-one-year-old daughter Susan left through a hole in the fence at about eight a.m. They later learned that the SS came a few hours after they left, shot anyone too old or sick to make the trip and marched the rest to Mauthausen.

Who were these folk and what had they done to deserve such treatment? Let's look at who the family were before checking out the adventures which had brought Clara thus far and adventures yet in store. In doing so, I have been able to trace the family only as far as the mid 1800s.

Karoly Krausz and His Descendants

When Hungarian gypsy musicians are not making their violins cry they are making them dance to the lively tunes of the csardas folk dance. This dance is named after the tavern, the csarda, where they originated.

Karoly (Carl or Charles) Kraus was relaxing in the csarda of the village where he was the local policeman in the Bakony area of Hungary, some distance south-west of Budapest and to the north of Lake Balaton. Karoly had been born in 1831 in Papa, a town a little west of where he now sat. He was Jewish, although it was unusual for a Jew in those days to hold such a responsible position. Nevertheless, he was well thought of in his public office, 'even if he was a Jew'.

He may have been relaxing in the csarda but a policeman is never completely off duty and he pricked up his ears when he heard a stranger begin to chat up the innkeeper's daughter, who was serving at the bar. That area at that time was infested with bandits, some of whom achieved considerable notoriety, as for example Robin Hood or Dick Turpin had in England or Ned Kelly in Australia. Ever the alert policeman, his suspicions had been aroused.

Over the next little while, he made sure he was in the csarda at the time of day that this stranger now regularly visited and made advances to the barmaid. As time went by, Carl overheard him subtly getting information from the girl about her father's money and valuables.

Carl discovered that he was indeed a bandit, the leader of a gang, and his purpose in leading the girl on was to gain information with which to plan a robbery. Using the information he had gathered, Carl mobilised the other police, foiled the robbery and, after a long and arduous chase, personally arrested the culprit and brought him in. Carl was hailed as a hero and received honours for his capture of the infamous bandit.

A closer look at Carl gives us some understanding of those times, an understanding which remains relevant today. Carl came from a strict orthodox Jewish family in Papa, a Hungarian town with a very large Jewish population at the time. Although I have described him as a policeman my understanding is that this job was a branch of the military. This was a problem as soldiers may of necessity have to eat whatever food may be available. Strict orthodox Jews may eat only Kosher hence Carl's decision to enlist and possibly have to eat non-Kosher food meant that he was disowned by his strictly religious father and never returned to Papa again in his life.

It is not clear whether joining up meant he had to, at least officially, renounce his Jewish roots and become a Christian but it is noted that his youngest child, my grandfather Fulop, became a Jewish cantor.

This issue causes internal friction in Israel to this day in that for this very reason the ultra-orthodox Jews of Israel are exempt from military service. As Israel has been under constant attack from its neighbours since its inauguration, one group refusing to take part in its defence understandably causes some issues.

Carl distinguished himself during his military career, winning many decorations including for saving 2 little girls from drowning. His capture of this bandit was the high point and he was highly decorated by the emperor for it. However he was wounded in this skirmish, losing an eye, and was invalided out of the service.

He moved to the city of Nagyszombat, now Trnava in Slovakia, where he met and married Neta Elbert. I am unsure whether this was his first or second marriage. Somewhat paradoxically considering that he had lost an eye, he became an optician and sold spectacles. According to one source he died on 5th May 1887 but according to my uncle Theo's (Tivi's,) memoirs he died when his youngest son, my grandfather, was 9 years old, which would make it 1885 or 1886. The couple had 5 children.

Of these the youngest was Fulop (Philip) my grandfather, born on 9 September 1876 (died 1952 in Casablanca, Morocco.) Fulop became a cantor, a Jewish worship leader in the chanting of prayers. He left Papa to take up a position as such in the synagogue at a town then called Beszterce Banya (*banya* is the Hungarian word for mine) somewhat to the north. His second son, my father, was born there in 1905.

My father was born in what was Hungary at the time but he became a Czech citizen when, after World War I, the agreements of the Versailles Treaty of 1919 reduced Hungary, a part of the former Austro-Hungarian empire, down to something like half its previous area. Beszterce Banya became Banska

Bystrica in what was then the newly formed country of Czechoslovakia. It is now in Slovakia.

Unfortunately, shifting borders were not the only characteristic of those times. With the political instability and Hitler's rise to power, anti-Semitism and other associated racism and intolerance, although nothing new, were rearing their ugly heads, as can be seen when we look at the fate of all too many members of the family tree.

Frida married a man called Henrich Elbert. We have no records today to explain why his surname was the same as Neta's maiden name. However it is clear from Tivi's memoirs that the Elbert family was a large one and closely associated with the Krausz family. In his memoirs Tivi several times refers to his cousin Carl Elbert and mentions the help given by the Elbert family in Fulop's upbringing and education after his father Carl's death. We surviving members of the family, a couple of generations down, are unclear on the details of the relationship between the two families but the following delightful incident which occurred in Sydney somewhere around the late 1950s confirms the relationship:Apparently, my uncle Tivi (Theo), my father's younger brother, was attending the *shul* (synagogue) in Sydney's eastern suburbs, where he saw a man who looked just like his uncle, with whom he had long ago lost contact. It turned out that this gentleman, Mr Elbert, was his long- lost uncle!

Although we are not sure of the exact relationship, we kids of my generation well remember Jeno (Eugene) Elbert and his wife. He had a well-developed, if sometimes bawdy sense of humour, and I remember his wife well, as she was always very kind to me. She was his second wife, his first wife and children having perished in the Holocaust. She had a son about my age or a tad younger by her first husband, who had also perished at the hands of the Nazis.

Back to Frida: we know nothing more about her except that the Nazis murdered both her and her husband but we don't know where or when.

Carl and Netta's second child was a boy, Zsigmund, who died young. Their third was also a girl, Mina. Mina married Moricz (Maurice) Taub, a Russian Jew and also a cantor. Together with their two children, Carla and Leo, the Taubs emigrated to New York in 1921, thus establishing the American branch of the family, a move that would be of importance to us later.

The full story is worth telling.

Moricz Taub was a Russian Jew from Minsk who trained as a cantor and migrated to Hungary before the first World War. He got a position in Budapest and married Mina, my great aunt, the older sister of my grandfather Fulop. The couple had a daughter, Carla, and a son, Leo.

As he spoke fluent Russian and German Moricz was recruited by the Austro-Hungarian Army as a spy and sent to Denmark where he was based in their headquarters in Copenhagen. One day he got to the office early when there was no-one else there yet and found a telegram which had just arrived ordering his superiors to get rid of him as he was considered unreliable. He did not return home but went straight to the port, found a ship to America and worked his passage to New York as a stoker. He had a good voice, found a large congregation and in no time at all was doing very well as a cantor.

The Hungarians thought he had been eliminated and gave my great aunt Mina with her 2 children, Carla and Leo, a war widow's pension. One day Mina's younger brother, my grandfather Fulop, received a postcard from the Red Cross informing him that his brother in law Moricz was alive and well in New York! According to my uncle Tivi's memoirs Moricz sent for his family "after the war." According to information I had from my late second cousin Gilbert, Carla's son, they emigrated in 1921. Moricz by then had a 3 story home for his reunited family.

Carla married Leo Brody, a furniture retailer in Pittsburgh. Thus their son Gilbert is my second cousin. Leo Taub married, had a son Richard, now deceased, then divorced and married Ruth, but they had no children.

My wife Heather and I met Leo and Ruth Taub in the early 1970s when they visited Australia, and we caught up again with Ruth, by then widowed, many years later when we visited New York before her death from cancer. She was one feisty lady. After Leo's passing and in her seventies, she took up not only travel, for example to Antarctica, but also competitive ballroom dancing, a pastime at which she excelled to the point of becoming number eight in the whole US!

Carl and Netta's other child was a daughter, Katherine. All we know of her is that she married a gentleman called Springer, also a cantor, and that they too both perished in the Holocaust.

The youngest was my grandfather Fulop.

Fulop Krausz and His Descendants

In Hungarian, the word *bacsi*, pronounced 'ba-chi' (short 'i') literally means 'uncle' but is applied, as far as children are concerned, to most older gentlemen. It is also used generally to refer affectionately to an elderly man, an *oreg bacsi*. Thus, although Philip Kraus (Krausz Fulop) was actually my paternal grandfather, he was Fulop *bacsi* to me.

Fulop married a lady called Jolan Partos and, as will become evident, the families became very intertwined shortly thereafter. Fulop and Jolan had six children. It was a very balanced family, three boys and three girls. The oldest, also Karoly, was born in 1904 and was followed a year later by my father, Imre, born in 1905.

I don't know much about Karoly. Obviously named after his grandfather I believe he had been married and divorced and at one time served in the army. At one point during World War II, he was staying with my maternal grandparents in Budapest. He went out to do some shopping, it may have been to buy some eggs, and never returned.

The Hungarian Nazis, the Nyilas or Arrow Cross, were if anything worse than their German SS counterparts. Before the war, Hungary, and especially Budapest, had a very large Jewish population. The persecution was so bad that it was estimated that in 1944 a Jew in rural Hungary had a less than ten per cent chance of surviving the next twelve months and a Jew in Budapest fifty per cent Thus we were fortunate not to have lost more of the family.

There is now a memorial on the bank of the Danube, just a little south of the Budapest Parliament House. The memorial is in the form of numerous pairs of shoes, men's, women's and children's, cast in bronze representing the shoes removed from the Jewish people lined up on the riverbank right there and shot so their bodies fell into the Danube.

The next child was a girl, Livia, known as Lilli (1906–2004.) She was followed in 1908 by a third boy, Tivadar (Tivi or Theo, 1908–1999). The last two were girls, Gabriella, 'Elli' (1910–2011) and Anna, 'Nushi' (1916–2011).

Due to the interactions of the families at this point, it is now time to temporarily leave the Krauses and have a look at Clara's family, the Elfers.

The Elfers and Partoses

In the first half of the nineteenth century, a gentleman called Michael Weisz married a lady called Gerle Singer. They had a daughter, Kati (1852–1924). Kati married Samuel Partos, originally Pollak (1851– 1924). They had four children. The first two were girls, Hermin and Yolan. We believe Hermin (1880–1953) was the elder but we are not sure. Jolan died in Casablanca in 1951. Their third child was also a girl, Yanka (1886–1944), and their fourth a boy, Jeno (Eugene) (1898– 1974). Jeno married Elizabeth Frankl and it was they and their daughter Susan (1924–2020) who were with Clara and her children in the camp and escaped from there together with them.

Of the older two Partos girls, Hermin married a gentleman called Odon (Edmund) Elfer in 1900. Their first son, Laszlo (Leslie), was born in 1901, their second son, Andor, in 1904. We have already learnt that Andor perished in one of Mauthausen's satellite camps the day before it was liberated. Ten years after Andor, on 4 January 1914, their daughter Clara, my mother, was born.

Odon Elfer (24 Sept 1876-22 May 1946) worked as an executive, possibly a paymaster, in the MAG factory, Hungary's largest vehicle manufacturer at the time and still in existence today. He was much loved by all, being honest and reliable in his work and compassionate to the employees. I understand he would even help them out from his own pocket on occasion. I still have some small decorative statuettes given to him, possibly on his retirement, in appreciation.

First son Les, who later became an engineer, was an adventurous lad and despite the difficult and risky times for a young man to be travelling in Europe just after World War I, off he went to find his fortune. Not much is known about his wanderings but he had converted to Catholicism and among other places visited Rome. He died of leukaemia in 1957. Nothing is known of Les's first marriage, which ended in divorce. He later married Martha Veg and quite some time later my cousin Istvan (Stephen in English but known to the family by the very diminutive 'Pisti') entered the scene on 4 July 1943.

We are now reminded that Hermin's sister Yolan had married Fulop Kraus and they had six children. These two sisters, Hermin and Yolan, decided the money (what money?) should stay in the family, so organised for Yolan and Fulop's son Imre, my father, to marry Clara, Hermin and Odon's daughter, and for Yolan's oldest daughter, Lilli, to marry Hermin's second son Andor. Apparently, first cousin marriages were not unusual in the European Jewish community of those times.

Andor and Lilli had a son, John (1935–2009), and a daughter, Anne (1936–2004).

At about the time of his marriage, Odon Elfer had bought an apartment on the third floor of a residential building at 7 Hernad *utca* (street) in district VII, Budapest. He later moved downstairs to an apartment on the first floor (second floor to Americans). This is the apartment to which my mother, baby brother and I initially returned after our escape from the camp and where I remember living before our emigration to Australia. It is in what was the Jewish quarter of Budapest and was little better than a ghetto during the war.

So those are the principal players.

Tivi became an architect and town planner of some note and was responsible for a lot of the subsequent town planning of Banska Bystrica. He changed his name to Karas, as that was more a Czech- sounding name. He married Susan Kardos. Susan had lost her first husband to the Holocaust. They had one daughter, my cousin Sylvia, born in 1946. They joined us in Australia in 1949.

Imre and Klari

My parents married, as arranged by their mothers, on 9 April 1935. (I did not come along until 1942.)

As has already been mentioned, Fulop and Yolan Kraus had six children. That was a lot to feed on a cantor's salary. It has also already been mentioned that the Partos family, of which both my grandmothers were members, had another daughter, Yanka.

Yanka had married a businessman called Zsigmund Eisler. The Eislers were childless so for economic reasons as well as to ease the family size at such a time of political unrest, when my father was thirteen he and his older brother Karoly went to live with their aunt and uncle in Szabadka/Subotica. Uncle Zsiga was a very prosperous businessman. Apart from the cement products factory he had a timberyard, a building supplies outlet and other business interests.

In his memoirs my uncle Tivi, Dad's younger brother, does not paint a very favourable picture of their aunt Yanka. Once he finished his schooling Karoly, said to be ungrateful and disrespectful to his aunt, returned to Banska Bystrica where he got a job in a timberyard. At the age of 20 he had to do compulsory military service in Moravia and as we have learnt he was at some stage married and divorced and later disappeared from the streets of Budapest. I have a photograph of my father as a young man in military uniform. I am guessing that he would have had to do the same.

My understanding is that when he reached adulthood, Dad worked as a representative for the concrete products factory and when he married, he and Clara, my mum, lived in the Yugoslav capital Belgrade, where Dad was in business for himself in some form of industrial chemistry. I assume that it was from this that he originally had the formula for the rust prevention and treatment product he later manufactured and sold in Australia as Ferropro. Ferropro was the first such product ever available in this country.

There was a complicated political situation in which Yugoslavia, as it then was, was trying to be neutral but was surrounded by increasingly hostile Axis countries – that is, those allied to Nazi Germany. Eventually, Germany persuaded Yugoslavia to join them but Hitler did not trust Yugoslavia and he ordered the Luftwaffe to bomb Belgrade on 6 April 1941. (Belgrade was later also bombed by the Allies on 16–17 April 1944.)

This was all about a year before I was born. As I remember the story told to me, my mother was at the markets when the bombers came over. Everybody was fleeing the city and she joined them. When she returned after the bombing was over, she found that a bomb had gone through their apartment and the only item rescued was a cast-iron cooking pot which subsequently continued to be used by my family, us included, for many years. Its enamel has now deteriorated beyond being usable but I have kept it as a memento and heirloom.

It is now on display at the Queensland Holocaust Museum in Brisbane. Apparently my father was in the bath at the time but fortunately was unhurt.

My parents then returned to live in Subotica, although my mother went back to Budapest for my birth.

From Subotica to Austria

So there we were in Szabadka/Subotica. As the Nazis' influence grew, Jewish men, including my father and an acquaintance Joe Fisher, were intermittently sent for variable lengths of time on forced labour. Joe later married my mother's cousin Susan Partos. The photograph I have of the labour group shows the men and their German guards pretty relaxed. Presumably this laid-back atmosphere could not have lasted under the circumstances.

Dad told me very little about his wartime experiences but he did say that at the end they were so hungry they ate grass and snails. When some of our family visited the forced labour camp site in 2017, we saw a number of disgusting-looking slugs all over the grass. I really felt for my poor father and the others with him, reduced to such hunger that they ate even these. As already related, when they got to the point that they could no longer work. they were sent to Mauthausen for extermination.

Dad did say that he got a fright one day when a family called Krausz arrived at the camp. He felt that if it were indeed us, we would all be doomed. It was not us but another family with that not uncommon name. My mother tells that somehow Dad heard of Paul's birth and also of our escape but did not know we had reached safety. The news gave him hope to carry on.

Dad also told me how towards the end of his time in Mauthausen he had what he described as 'crocodile skin'. When I became a medical student, I realised that he most likely had pellagra, a vitamin deficiency disease. He also had, from his description, a severe abscess on the back of his neck. He says the Americans operated on him and nursed him back to health.

Meanwhile my mother, now pregnant with my brother, and I were in Szabadka/Subotica, staying at the accommodation provided by Uncle Szigmund and Aunt Yanka. Susan Fisher and her parents Jeno and Elizabeth Partos were also in Subotica, Jeno being Yanka's younger brother.

The Nazis evicted us from our accommodation and gave it to some peasant folk who really did not appreciate or look after it. We were sent to the Subotica ghetto, from where we were to be deported to Auschwitz for extermination.

I am not sure of the exact dates here. I have a photograph taken to mark my second birthday in June 1944. It is a professional studio portrait with me dressed up for the occasion like the proverbial Little Lord Fauntleroy and I presume means that we were not yet in the ghetto. Susan Fisher tells me that we were in the ghetto for only a very short time, a few weeks. This is consistent with us not being there yet on my second birthday in June and being on our way to the camp on 11 July as Susan records.

From the ghetto, people were deported in trains of cattle trucks to Auschwitz for extermination. I am not totally clear of the events that occurred when it was our turn, having had to piece together the various fragments of stories I have heard. I have no conscious memories of the events, although I have come to realise that many of the things that have troubled me later in life are from half remembered early childhood memories of those times.

We, my mother and myself, the Partos family of three and Uncle and Aunt Eisler were in a queue to be loaded onto a train. I think I remember my mother saying that she went to the aid of an elderly man whom she vaguely knew. He was blind and in great distress and in going to his aid we changed to a different queue. Another version I have heard is that someone advised us to change queues. At any rate, we did change the line in which we were. The Partoses came with us but the Eislers stayed where they were. As a consequence, they perished at Auschwitz.

Having changed queues, we were loaded into the rear of the train and that is what saved us. The Allies have been criticised that they did not act on requests to bomb the railway tracks leading to the concentration camps. That would have saved countless Jewish lives. Their rationale was that they were putting all their efforts into fighting and winning the war, which also no doubt saved numerous Jewish lives.

Nevertheless, what saved us was that the train went over a bridge which had been bombed. Whether the Eislers were on an earlier train that had passed that point before the bridge was destroyed, whether the bridge was bombed, or failed as a result of the bombing, while our train was partway over it, I don't know, but the train, or the rear of it where we were, was not able to proceed to Auschwitz because the bridge was out. And that is how we came to be at the labour camp instead of Auschwitz.

I think my mother told us that we were in transit on the train for a total of about nine days.

The local pharmacist at Subotica was also Jewish. My mother knew him and his wife, and being a trained dressmaker and corsetière, she made clothes for the pharmacist's wife and was on close first name terms with her.

In a coincidence reminiscent of my uncle Tivi finding his long-lost uncle in Sydney, when Heather and I lived and worked in Townsville in the late 1990s and early 2000s, I was introduced to Andrew, who like me was a Jewish follower of Jesus. We had never met before but it turned out that Andrew was the son of the Subotica pharmacist.

Like us, he and his family were in the Subotica ghetto and put on a train to Auschwitz. In their case, they were in the last two carriages. As I understand was made well known by the movie *Schindler's List*, various Jewish industrialists paid large sums of money to the Germans to ransom at least some of the Jews who were otherwise headed for the extermination camps. Andrew and his family were among the lucky ones. They ended up in a forced labour camp in Vienna, working for the Siemens electrical factory.

So we had been little kids together in the same town, our parents had known each other, we had been in the same ghetto and deported for the same reason and to the same destination; and we first met six decades later on the other side of the world in the remote rural city of Townsville.

Further information about the train

Since writing the original edition I have had two lots of information from Mr Miki Granski, the grandson of Dr Balog, the doctor at the camp.

Miki's first bit of information was to the effect that the locomotive pulling the train was not a very powerful one and from time to time, when encountering difficult parts of the track, had to take the train piecemeal, a couple of carriages at a time. It was on one of these occasions, when the locomotive was taking the carriages two by two over a bridge that the bridge was bombed and the locomotive could not complete the job.

The bombing is what Mum's cousin Susan Fisher told of and the smaller locomotive needing to take the train piecemeal explains why our having gone to another carriage via changing queues saved us.

However, subsequent to receiving this information from Miki, he discovered his late mother's diary and was able with some difficulty to decipher it and get it translated. Miki makes the point very strongly that his mother was an avid diarist, keeping a contemporaneous diary even at the most difficult of times. He is adamant about the accuracy of the information in the diary and the diary contains no mention whatever of either the train or any bridge being bombed!

This raises the question of why we then did not proceed to Auschwitz and certain death. Miki suggests the possibility that this may have been due to the intervention of that controversial character Rudolf Kastner, although obviously we were not on the (in)famous Kastner train, which went to freedom in Switzerland via Bergen-Belsen (sic). Dr Balog and his two daughters were in the same two rear carriages as us.

Life in the Camp

There was a doctor, Ernst Balog, who was also an inmate of the camp. He did what he could for the inmates although of course he had no facilities or equipment. He attended my mother when she gave birth to my brother Paul.

Dr Balog had two teenage daughters who were also in the camp with us. I understand that the girls used to mind us children when the adults were busy. They would teach and tell stories, although I do not remember that.

Food was not plentiful. Apparently, Uncle Jeno *bacsi* worked in the kitchen and was able to bring back potato peelings. That doesn't sound like much but every little helped, not to mention that we later learned that that is the most nutritious part of a potato.

Some time back, Dr Balog's grandson, Miki Granski, the son of Dr Balog's older daughter, contacted me. He was actually looking for my brother Paul, whom his grandfather had delivered, as he was researching Dr Balog's story. In 2010, shortly after Miki made contact, my wife Heather and I visited Israel. Miki's mother had passed away by then but his aunt, Olga Dothan, was still alive and living in a retirement home in Tel Aviv. Miki came down from Haifa where he lived and we all met at Olga *neni*'s place. (*Neni* is aunt in Hungarian, the feminine version of *bacsi*.) Olga *neni* remembered me as a child. We had not met for sixty-five years. It was a wonderful and very emotional reunion.

The following is taken from a letter written by my aunt Susan Fisher (Partos) to Miki Granski as she tells the story first-hand. I have added some further notes in plain text where relevant.

Dear Miki,

I arrived with my parents, Yeno and Elizabeth Partos, at Strasshof [a suburb twenty-five kilometres east of Vienna] on 11th July 1944, my late mother's birthday. We slept in an old cemetery on the first night and the next day, to the best of my recollection, we were taken to Viehofen [about seventy kilometres west of Vienna]. None of us had our heads shaved.

There was a POW camp adjacent to our camp and the two camps were separated by a dirt road and as there was no fence surrounding our camp we were able to go across to the POWs. There were French and Belgian POWs at the camp but I don't recall any Jugoslavs. They occasionally gave us cigarettes, which we traded for bread with your grandfather.

It was along this dirt road that we walked daily for about 30 minutes until we reached our work site, which was on the banks of the Traisen. Our project was to build a levy on the bank to prevent the river flooding in the spring. The levy was built up with dirt that was brought there by a trolley. This proved to be ineffectual as the river broke its banks regardless.

Whilst working on the riverbank we would sometimes hear someone whistle and we would look across to see someone disappear into the forest and we would go over and find that they had left some food for us.

I do not remember anyone being shot at the camp. The first person to die in our hut was Izso P and he died from a bleeding ulcer.

The Lagerfuher's [camp commandant's] name was Kubitchek and he was a Nazi and wore a feather in his hat. There were two old Austrian guards who were more humane and their names were Seif and Losleben. Losleben's son was in the army and when he returned on leave, he gave some baby clothes to Paul's mother. She kept this a secret for obvious reasons and we only learned of this after the war.

It says a lot for both old Herr Losleben and his son that they did this. Had they been discovered, they would have been shot. Without their bravery and kindness, we would have been in big trouble indeed, as Mum had absolutely nothing for the baby, no clothes, nappies, bottles... nothing. I understand that the younger Losleben visited my grandparents in Budapest to get these items. It must have given them a fright to have a German soldier knock on their door! The goods were smuggled bit by bit to my mother by Losleben. I only found out about this later in life and have no idea how to contact the Loslebens or their descendants but would love to have the opportunity to thank them.

Kubitchek had an affair with one of the girls at the camp and when she became pregnant, your grandfather arranged for her to have an abortion.

Seif 'befriended' a girl called M.K., who was sixteen at the time, and he supplied food for her that she gave to her father. She lives in Sydney and I contacted her but she doesn't want to be involved in your project. She started crying and became very distressed when I approached her about it.

Susan does not mention here that although Sief and Losleben were humane, there were visits from the SS from time to time and they were not. On one of their visits, they decided to blame Dr Balog for the death from dysentery of one of the inmates and had him flogged and made the whole camp – men, women and children – watch. I have no conscious memory of this but when I learnt of it, I realised that it explained some of the hang-ups I have had throughout my life.

I also understand that Susan and maybe some others may have made occasional trips to the nearby village of Viehofen to get bread and milk.

Losleben warned Clara Kraus, who is my cousin and is Paul's mother, that we would all be moved to Mauthausen and she asked that we go with her and her two children into the woods and towards the Russian front. The Russians were getting closer and as we walked there were hundreds of American bombers flying overhead and dropping leaflets as well as spiral-shaped streamers which were made of some kind of metal foil that I think was intended to interfere with radio communications or radar.

Susan is correct. They were dropping strips of foil, codename Window, to confuse the German radar.

My father was pushing a wheelbarrow that contained our meagre possessions and as he crossed the river on the narrow plank that we had to walk across, he overbalanced and fell in, wheelbarrow and all. He retrieved the wheelbarrow and some of our possessions with the help of a couple who were there, but most things were lost.

This couple now joined us and we arrived at a small village where we sheltered in a half-built house with no roof. We realised that we could not spend the night there with two young children, so we continued towards the village. The other couple, whose name was Schaffer, stayed there and we later learned that they had been shot.

When we finally arrived in Budapest, we were told about JOINT. This was an aid organisation that was established by American Jews to help survivors. The first person that we saw when we went to JOINT was the son of the Schaffers. We told him that we had been at the camp with his parents but could not bring ourselves to tell him that they had died.

On our way to the village, we came to a monastery and decided it would be a good place to seek refuge. As we walked through the gate, we found ourselves in a huge estate. The grounds were occupied by German soldiers and camouflaged artillery. We could not about turn, so we continued towards the monastery. The nuns took us in and that evening we had dinner in the kitchen, with them and the German soldiers!

The next morning, Clara Kraus decided to tell the Mother Superior that we were Jewish and so she made us leave but did not betray us to the Germans. We then continued walking towards the village, towards the Russian front. The road was filled with refugees who were all walking in the opposite direction away from the Russians.

We reached the village and in the first house that we approached, there was a woman alone with her daughter. She let us stay and the next morning the Russians arrived and my father was able to talk to them in mixture of Serb and Russian, which saved them (and us) from being robbed or raped.

Susan omits some relevant parts here, probably because they are distressing for her. Her father Jeno *bacsi*'s ability to converse with the Russian commander kept us safe. I understand that the Russian soldiers, a pretty wild lot, raped every woman and girl in that village except in the household that put us up. Susan to this day shudders and nearly cries whenever she tells the story of the screaming she heard continuing through the night.

Anxious to move on, we started walking back along the way we had come, now behind the Russians, on the road to Vienna. As we passed the monastery, we saw that it had been bombed and completely destroyed!

Along the way, farmers let us shelter in their barns as well as giving us food and milk. Then the Soviets helped us by giving us food and transporting us on their trucks until we reached the Vienna woods. From there, they went back for more supplies.

We then travelled with other survivors on mostly coal trains or any other trains that were going in the direction of Budapest.

My mother tells this story of the journey home in very similar terms. We hitched rides on Russian army trucks and freight trains going in the right general direction. At one place, some women near the tracks had a large pot of soup from which they fed people such as us returning from deportation. I can't remember whether my mother said the journey took us nine days or two weeks. She thought it was rather a long time but learnt later that it was a bit of a record quick time. For comparison, the distance from Vienna to Budapest by road is 243 kilometres, under three hours' drive and a similar time by train!

Clara found her mother in their old apartment in Budapest and stayed there with her two children and I continued to Subotica with my parents.

Postscript to Susan Fisher's story

My mother told the story that once, while we were wandering around the countryside after escaping from the camp, an American plane swooped down very low, so low that she saw the pilot, who waved to us. She said that he was black.

When years later she told me this, I, being very much into aircraft, especially World War II aircraft, asked her what type of plane it was. Frustratingly, although not unexpectedly, she didn't know. It was just 'a plane'.

Some time after that, I learnt the story of the Tuskegee Airmen and realised that this could only have been one of their P51 Mustangs, as they were the only African American pilots in the US Air Force. As it was April 1945, it would have been a P51D, as the Tuskegee Airmen had had their P51Bs replaced by the D model before that time.

When Heather and I visited the huge airshow at Oshkosh in 2002, the Tuskegee Airmen's Association had a tent there. At that time, a few of the original Tuskegee Airmen were still alive. (Their children and grandchildren now keep their memory alive.) I spoke with one of them and told him the story. He didn't know who the pilot concerned was but, for all he and I knew, it might even have been him.

Other family during the war years

As mentioned earlier, Budapest, indeed all Hungary, was a most dangerous place for Jews by 1944. It had been better earlier in the war when some Jews from places like Germany and Austria even sought refuge there. As already mentioned, my uncle Karoly, staying in my maternal grandparents' Hernad utca apartment went out to buy some eggs and never returned.

My uncle Andor, the younger of Mum's 2 older brothers, owned a factory making polishes. One of his employees lived in the outer suburb of Kobanya and when things became too dangerous in Budapest city kindly took in the whole family and hid them. That also included Mum's older brother Laszlo, his wife Marti and their son, my cousin Pisti, who lived in an apartment overlooking the Danube. Again we have an act not only of great kindness but also of great courage should their benefactor have been betrayed.

I remember my cousin John, 9 years old at the time, telling me he received the news as he finished up at school one day and instead of going home walked the 8+km to Kobanya. John, being 7 years my senior, had conscious memories of life in Budapest during the war and remembered having to wear the yellow star and the taunting and abuse that came with it.

My paternal grandparents, Dad's younger brother Tivi, Dad's 2 younger sisters, one with husband and daughter, the other, Nusi, still single at this stage, were in Slovakia. Things were far from safe and peaceful and they had to move house but were then able to stay in the same place, Tivi says in his memoirs "until after the war" but it is clear that at some point they had to flee, I gather with the collapse of the Slovak uprising in late 1944. The Slovak uprising was second only to the Warsaw uprising. It lasted 2 months but was doomed to failure

Tivi was working as an architect and town planner for the council, although not surprisingly there was not much work. One evening as Tivi was walking along the street there was an air raid siren and all the lights went out. Some planes went over but did not seem to bomb the town but headed over a nearby hill. The next day when he went to inspect a building, the construction of which he was supervising, he saw a workman whom he did not recognise.

Although the man was doing a menial task he gave the appearance of being intelligent and well educated. He gave Tivi advice to get out and instructions as to the necessary equipment etc needed to do so. He had been parachuted in the night before, when the sirens had gone off, to perform this task. His name was Dubcek and his son Alexander later became the famous Slovak statesman. Tivi many times recounted with pride his friendship and association with Alexander Dubcek although this association was not political but based on his wartime meeting with Dubcek's father. Tivi credits Dubcek senior with saving the lives of himself and family and many others through his timely warning.

They all got out to villages nearby where, associated with partisans, they lived in hiding in bunkers they had dug out, for the remainder of the war.

I am not quite sure of the story but Dad and Tivi's youngest sister Nusi did end up in a concentration camp, I think Auschwitz, which fortunately she survived.

After the war Tivi married Susan, nee Kardos, whom he had met earlier. At the time Tivi first met her she had been married to her first husband. Less than 3 weeks after their marriage he was taken by the Nazis and a couple of years later Susan learnt that he had died of typhus in a forced labour camp. When Susan attended a family reunion after the war, of about 70 members of her large extended family, 50 were missing.

Life in Postwar Europe

Szabadka/Subotica

My mother, baby brother Paul and I stayed for a short while with my maternal grandparents in the apartment on the first floor of 7 Hernad *utca* in Budapest, then we went back to Szabadka/Subotica.

At this time, Mum did not know whether or not Dad was still alive or where he was. She then got word from someone that he had survived and would be back in due course and she looked out for him every day until one day he turned up, gaunt and lost-looking. It was some months before he recovered enough to work.

Heather and I visited Mauthausen in 2000. It was a very emotive feeling of unreality. There we were on a very beautiful day in the most glorious countryside, Mauthausen actually being a lovely, very picturesque village. Yet on its outskirts was this camp in which, for all the beauty of its setting, the most dreadful horrors were perpetrated. It has been cleaned up and only two or three dormitory huts remain. It was an indescribably unreal feeling to realise Dad had been there. I don't want to go back.

I learnt a lesson when we visited Mauthausen. Before going in, we were standing in the front courtyard outside the main gate, where buses now park. I was trying to cope with the flood of emotions as I took in the surroundings. The only other people there were a French family, the patriarch a diminutive elderly man whose granddaughter, a pretty little blonde girl, was running around on the walkway above the gates where the Nazi iron eagle had been.

The little Frenchman came up to me for a chat and I told him my father had been there at the time of its liberation. He pointed out a photo to me. It showed a group of newly released inmates pulling the Nazi iron eagle down with a rope, like a tug-of-war team. Just in the picture at the back of this group was a little guy in a raincoat with a white stripe on his sleeve. That was him. At age sixteen he was active in the French Resistance, had been caught by the Nazis and escaped from several concentration camps. He was at Mauthausen when it was liberated.

My first reaction at seeing the little girl running around was that it was inappropriate. I changed my mind rapidly when he told me his story. What triumph he must have felt to see his little granddaughter playing where once the Nazis had tried to eliminate him!

New insight about the Frenchman

When seeking permission to use the photo of Mauthausen after liberation (page 223), René Bienert, who is responsible for the Photo Collections at Mauthausen Memorial, was kindly able to identify this gentleman as Pierre Serge Choumoff (1921-2012). He had previously been in Gusen concentration camp and after the war, testified as a witness in war crime trials and published research papers on the murder of prisoners with poison gas. Mr Bienert was able to supply the following account provided by Mr Choumoff: *When we heard of the arrival of the first Americans in the camp, the entire roll-call area started moving. I recall that with some French comrades, I made my way to the main gate to obtain weapons from the Kommandantur. Then I went to the Garagenhof, where I saw a group of inmates, mostly Spaniards, trying to pull down the eagle. I put my rifle down and joined them. I wanted to be part of this symbolic act at all costs. I can still remember how difficult it was, and several of us had to pull on the rope. Finally, the eagle toppled to the ground and broke into pieces. I can see myself in the photo taken at the time wearing the piece of striped cloth on my back and trouser leg to indicate that I was an inmate of Gusen.* (Mauthausen Memorial: das sichtbare unfassbare – the visible part. Katalog zur gleichnamigen Wanderausstellung, Wien 2024, p. 140)

At some stage, I am not sure whether in Budapest immediately on our return, whether during our stay then in Szabadka or whether during our stay in Budapest before emigrating, my infant brother Paul developed meningitis – no small thing now but even more serious then. I have been told this was the case but I don't personally remember it.

We are in possession of some valuables, artworks and such, which have been handed down in the family. I am not sure how these survived;

maybe some were with my grandparents in Budapest or Banska Bystrica (although I have no memories at all of Banska Bystrica and very few of my paternal grandparents). I think some had been hidden in Szabadka/Subotica in the rather optimistic hope that we would be able to go back for them. My mother was never very forthcoming with me in such matters and my Aunt Susan cannot recall where many of these things were from but is fairly sure that at least some had come from Uncle Zsigmond Eisler.

Although I was only about three or four years old, I do have some memories of Szabadka in those days. I have always been interested in aircraft. This must be in the DNA as I clearly remember one time when my brother and I were taken for a walk in the countryside near Szabadka and we went past an airfield. I can remember seeing numerous wrecked aircraft, I think fighter aircraft up on their noses and burnt-out, and my disappointment that there was not a single intact aircraft for me to admire.

The scenes of devastation we saw on our walk came back to me when, many years later in 1999, I was in the back of an RAAF truck en route from Kieta airstrip to our base at Loloho in Bougainville as part of the Australian Peace Monitoring Group, and looked out on the ravaged countryside following the horrible civil war that had devastated Bougainville for ten years.

I also remember playing with my brother on a hot summer day in a concrete tub of water; the tub no doubt a product of the factory. We splashed around and played with some tiny fish caught in the nearby creek. The fish did not survive.

Another time, my father bought a black pig at the market and brought it home. (My apologies to the sensitivities of any observant Jewish folk reading this!) As I remember it, Dad drove the pig home along the path from the market, guiding it with a stick. I presume it was of normal pig size but to a three-year-old that made it about the size of a hippopotamus to me. It seemed enormous. The only further thing I remember about the pig is that the butcher came and our shed had more sausages, salamis and wursts hanging in it than I can remember seeing before or since. (Except maybe at the Grand Market in Budapest six decades later.)

My mother told me that after some time we regained our proper old accommodation. Mum and Dad wound up the concrete products business and sold it and we moved to Budapest, back to my grandparents' in Hernad *utca* and I clearly remember living there. My Aunt Lilli, Dad's sister and the widow of Andor, my mother's brother, together with her two children, my cousins John and Anne Elfer, also lived with us in that small apartment.

Budapest

I remember the apartment reasonably well, especially that the pantry door was next to the toilet door and I always hoped that anyone relieving themselves during the night would go in the correct door.

I was in Budapest with my second son, Andrew, in 2007. We went to look at the old building. That style of building is in the form of a square with the accommodation around the outside and a central courtyard. When we visited the building, the entrance door to the courtyard was open, so we went in and the memories came flooding back.

I remembered a little yellow bicycle I had been given and kept downstairs in a corner of the yard. A gentleman seeing me with it asked me, with tongue in cheek, whether I had a flat tyre, to which I replied very seriously that I could not have a flat as the tyres were solid rubber.

There was also a staircase near the front entrance and another in the diagonally opposite corner. When Andrew and I had a closer look at the opposite one, I remembered it very clearly. Although it was not the one we usually used, I remember falling down it once, rolling uncontrollably bump, bump, bump, down the stairs to the bottom. Fortunately, little boys are resilient and the main thing hurt was my pride.

As Andrew and I looked up at our old apartment, we saw that the kitchen window was open and someone was moving around inside. I considered knocking on the door, introducing myself and asking if we could have a short look inside. I decided against it, partly as I was diffident due to my still very rusty Hungarian, but I think mainly because my emotions were too mixed up. I knew I would be sorry not to have asked and I was right, but that was the best I could cope with then.

Back to 1946 or 1947

Dad tidied up and sold Uncle Andor's business. I think it made polishes. I understand that Dad and his cousin and brother-in-law Andor had agreed that should one of them perish and the other live, the survivor would look after the deceased's wife (sister in either case). Dad did look after his sister Lilli very well, both then and later in Australia.

The business was called Elka and I remember they had a car. It was as well all was sold as Hungary, having been liberated by the Russians, became a communist country and all businesses were nationalised soon after. Grandpa Odon died in 1946.

I guess Dad was still very traumatised by his wartime experiences at that time. As a child, the only thing I picked up of his nervous manner, but a habit that irritated me, was that when the radio was on and he listened to music, as soon as the piece of music finished and the announcer came on, he would jump up and fiddle with the tuning dial until he found some more music, then when that piece of music finished and the announcer's voice came on, he would jump up and do the same.

I don't think that I was completely spared that way either. Children are affected by such experiences, perhaps as much as or more than adults, as at least adults can understand what is happening. My late cousin John, seven years my senior, had spent the war years in Budapest and being that much older than I had conscious memories of those times. He told me much later, when we were both older adults, that I had been an outgoing and talkative child until we were deported but was very quiet and said little on our return. I remember that I unfortunately wet the bed quite a lot.

I also sucked my thumb when going to sleep at night. My left thumb. This habit was only cured when, aged about nine, I fell off a scooter and suffered a rather nasty break of the left wrist. (A compound Smith's fracture, the opposite of a Colles', for those wanting to know.) I eventually had to have an open reduction of this and in those days the preparation for surgery involved wrapping my whole left forearm and hand up in a large bandage, presumably after washing with antiseptic. This went on for several days, so for a few nights I was unable to suck that thumb and never have since!

I also had some confused memories of the sleeping accommodation in the camp. My memory, as I thought, was of the sleeping arrangements on the *Derna*, the ship on which we came to Australia and where the men and women were segregated, even married couples and families. I clearly remembered multi-tiered bunks; not individual bunks but kind of like long shelves on each of which a number of people slept. The distance between the tiers of bunks was so little that even as a child I barely had room to sit up.

It was only many years later, watching a documentary on TV, that I realised that what I so clearly remembered was the sleeping quarters in the camp, not on the ship. Photos of these bunks can be found readily on the internet in a search for pictures taken in concentration camps and we actually saw some in the few cleaned-up and sanitised huts left standing at Mauthausen when we visited there in 2000.

That this left such an impression on my memory is interesting in that we can only have been in a communal hut in the camp for a short while as the commandant gave my mother a small separate hut in view of my brother's imminent birth.

I also have some claustrophobia and always sit in an aisle seat on a plane and at the end of the row in church or, whenever possible, in a theatre. I believe this comes from being crowded into the cattle trucks on the way to the camp. I am only now overcoming the more severe claustrophobia of this type that I get when at the end of a flight and before they open the aircraft door everybody stands up to get their bags from the overhead lockers to be ready to disembark. The large number of people crammed into that enclosed space is more evident then than when everyone is in their seats and it is sometimes all I can do to not panic before they open the door and people start to file out.

Another more amusing but somewhat embarrassing issue was the recurring nightmare I had for many years, I think until I realised its origin. The dream took different forms but the theme was always the same: I had to go to the toilet and either had to do so in public, or the walls or door of the toilet disappeared leaving me in full view. It took me a long time to realise that this probably harked back to the cattle trucks to the camps which had no facilities other than a bucket passed around at times. I also had more conventional nightmares fairly often for quite a long while as a child.

I have few other memories of life in Budapest at that time. I remember on one occasion in the winter we saw a snowman that someone had built and had used dollops of horse manure for buttons down the front. It's a long time now since horses were used in Budapest although when we first went back in 2000 and 2001 there were numerous little Trabant cars: 500cc two-cylinder, two-stroke, East German made and virtually extinct now.

Another aspect of life then was the arrival of parcels my parents referred to as *Ikka csomag* (*csomag* is parcel in Hungarian). These were aid parcels which I believe came from America. Susan Fisher has mentioned the Jewish aid agency called JOINT. I have tried to research Ikka or Ika but have drawn a blank. At any rate, these large parcels contained food and possibly other goods and were most welcome. I remember particularly enjoying some tinned meat.

I am not sure how often we got these parcels but do remember that when we got to Australia, my parents sent similar parcels to the folks still back home. Large parcels well wrapped and sewn into a calico outer covering.

Emigration: The trip to Sydney

After the horrors of the war, many people just wanted to get out of Europe and start a new life elsewhere, especially as Hungary had been liberated by and was under the control of Russia. Nor should it be forgotten that Europe had been the site of so much extremely vicious anti-Semitism for a very long time, culminating in Hitler's persecutions of the 1930s and in his 'final solution' of attempting to kill every Jew in Europe in the Holocaust.

I am not quite sure how we managed to get out of Hungary. My father was a Czech citizen due to the rearrangement of borders previously referred to, so that may have helped. There may also have been some greasing of palms but that is only a suspicion that came to mind just now. I really don't know.

I understand my parents paid a lot of money for those days, a thousand US dollars, to get somewhere in South America but the money disappeared and no more was heard. My father's cousin Leo Taub was in New York and I believe Dad made enquiries about going there, as I remember him telling Paul and me about the wonders of the buildings of New York which were so high that they called them skyscrapers. Whether we went to NY or Australia depended on which visa came through first.

We ended up coming to Australia, being sponsored by Balazs (Blaise) Nestel, an old school friend of Mum's older brother, who had emigrated before the war. The Nestels' younger son, Paul, did medicine and became a very noted cardiologist.

Apparently we had bought airline tickets, to be picked up in Paris. We duly caught the train on 15 August 1948, from the Keleti Palyaudvar (Eastern Railway Station) in Budapest, not far from Hernad *utca*.

We got to Paris but the tickets, which had been bought and paid for, did not exist. We must have stayed in Paris for a short time until we made some other arrangements to get to Australia. I managed to only wet the bed once there and remember the sheet being washed and draped over the chairs on the balcony of our hotel room to dry. Mum took a photo of what she believed was the Arc de Triomphe but was actually the Petite Arc de Triomphe at the other end of the Champs Elysée. I recognised it from her photo when we drove to Paris when I was on leave from my hospital training job in England in 1970 and 1971. Parts of Dad and me are in the bottom right-hand corner of Mum's photo. The camera, a Voigtlander, had belonged to my late uncle Bandi (Andor.) I still have it but it has a broken part now which cannot be repaired.

We were offered tickets on a 'luxury' liner, the *Derna*, leaving from Marseille on 30 August 1948. (It turned out to be a horror voyage that took until 5 November and is the subject of a book, *The Voyage of their Life*, by Diane Armstrong, who was a little girl with us on that voyage and grew up to be a journalist and author. It is a book that should be read by those reading this.)

We travelled to Marseille by train. At one of the railway stations, a kind stranger pressed a huge orange each into my brother Paul's and my hands. We had also been given some small toy paddles, red and green, which were replicas of what railway staff used to direct locomotives in railway yards. Paul and I stood at the open doorway of a railway carriage when our train was stopped in such a yard. We playfully signalled to the driver of a nearby locomotive and I think he humoured us, stopping and starting his locomotive on our signals.

The ship was overcrowded with more than its legal allotment of Jewish people. All had been caught up in the war. One man was said to have been a Nazi during the war, masquerading as a refugee to escape justice. Apparently he disappeared, presumably overboard, one night.

It was very hot coming through the tropics and the crew had set up a large tarpaulin on deck that they filled with water to make a quasi swimming pool. The ship kept on being delayed by breakdowns, the food was bad and families were separated as the men were segregated from the women and children.

I remember we got off for a land excursion at Colombo, Ceylon (now Sri Lanka). We took a tram to the zoo but were lucky to get there and back due to language difficulties. Not too many Sri Lankans in those times spoke Hungarian or German, in which my parents were fluent. My parents' English was at best rudimentary. To add to the confusion, my parents were under the impression that unlike everyone else the Ceylonese nodded for 'no' and shook their heads for 'yes'. Looking back on it, I don't think they were right but it didn't help at the time. At any rate, we did have a shore excursion and did make it back to the ship!

A lot of flying fish landed on the deck and on one occasion everyone lined the rail to look at a whale. To my disappointment, I could not see it. I probably didn't know what to look for.

My brother Paul celebrated his fourth birthday on board ship on 20 October 1948. We cannot have been too far from Fremantle by then as we went from Fremantle to Melbourne. Someone, I think it may have been the ship's baker, made a small birthday cake for Paul and they managed to find one candle to grace the cake. Their effort was much appreciated.

I remember the port at Fremantle as a collection of corrugated-iron sheds, a far cry from the beautiful boat harbour it is today. Due to the dreadful conditions on board the ship, some people originally bound for Melbourne got off at Fremantle and made their way overland, a more difficult undertaking then than it is today.

I did not realise until I read Diane Armstrong's book just how notorious that voyage had become. There were newspaper articles and all. Quite something for a small migrant ship arriving in Australia to make the major newspapers of the day.

We arrived in Melbourne on Friday 5 November 1948, the Friday of Melbourne Cup week, although my parents had no idea then, or to their dying days, what horseracing was about. We were to stay in Melbourne overnight and get tickets for the train to Sydney the following night.

Dad was a bit puzzled and perturbed by how quiet Melbourne was. After all, it was meant to be a major Australian city, second only to Sydney. Furthermore, they could not understand why it was so difficult to find accommodation for the night. All anybody could tell them was that 'It's the Melbourne Cup.' But a cup is something you drink out of, so what could a 'Melbourne Cup' be and why would it make accommodation so difficult to find?

We did eventually find a spot to lay our heads for the night and duly caught the train, the famous Spirit of Progress, the next day. Mum and

Dad were distressed to learn that we would have to change trains at Albury on the NSW border onto a NSW train, the Melbourne Limited Express. (This was due to Victorian trains running on broad gauge tracks, 5 feet 3 inches, 1,600mm, whereas NSW used the standard gauge of 4 feet 8½ inches, 1,435mm.) I remember them saying to each other that they would not let the family at home know, when they wrote their next letter, that we had had to change trains in the middle of the night. The track is standard gauge all the way now!

We were to stay with Balazs (Blaise) Nestel and his family at Canley Vale in Sydney's west. It's just a little north west of Prospect Reservoir, with which I became very familiar, at least from the air, many years later when I got my pilot's licence, as Prospect is an inbound reporting point for Bankstown Aerodrome. Being fairly dense I only recently realised that the area over which I flew so regularly while operating out of Bankstown was the cradle of our life in Australia.

So there we were at the Nestels' in the then outer Sydney suburb of Canley Vale. It was way out in the sticks in those days and the Nestels had a small farm. I remember Mrs Nestel (Erzsi *neni*, Auntie Elizabeth) showing me how she killed, plucked and cleaned a chook. The geese which wandered around dominated the place and terrorised everybody.

We were there about six weeks and then rented a cottage at 16 Tessa Street, Chatswood, which we subsequently bought and where we lived from early 1949 until we moved to East Roseville in 1955. My mother had become a Christian and although she said we were Presbyterian that church was on the other side of the busy Pacific Highway and St Paul's Church of England (now Anglican) was just up the road from us, so that's where we went and Paul and I went to Sunday school. The folk from there were very kind to us 'bloody refos' and they certainly appreciated the cakes Mum baked!

Paul and I attended Chatswood Central School, which is still there and looks much the same. I went on to North Sydney Boys' High School but when we moved to East Roseville, Paul was still in primary school and changed to Roseville School. I went on to Sydney University.

At East Roseville we were a couple of doors up from Edwards Tennis School, run by Victor A. Edwards, who subsequently took Evonne Goolagong-Cawley under his wing. We played tennis there with Dick Smith, who was also a schoolmate of Paul's at Roseville. Edwards Tennis School, to which everybody who was anybody went, even us as neighbours, had the Latin motto, I believe a quote from Julius Caesar, '*Veni, vidi, vici*,' which being translated is 'I came, I saw, I conquered.' We smart alec kids naturally translated it into 'Weeny, weedy and weaky.'

Other Family

Dad and Mum worked hard to bring the rest of the family out to Australia. Frico Frommer had taken his family – that is, his wife Nusi, Dad's youngest sister, and their two daughters Cathy and Eva – to Casablanca in Morocco, where Dad's parents, Fulop and Yolanda Kraus, joined them. They are buried there but when Morocco ceased to be a French colony, the Frommers moved to Spain. Another of Dad's sisters, Elli, had moved with her husband Bela Sip and daughter Vera Sipova to Casablanca, then Switzerland.

Hence Paul and I hardly know some of our cousins. Cathy Frommer visited Heather and me when we were in the UK and she had a trip to England in 1970. She was seventeen at the time and that is the only time we have seen her. Her younger sister Eva still lives in Switzerland, or between Madrid in Spain and Switzerland. We have never met but thanks to Facebook have recently got to know each other.

Heather and I met Dad's sister Elli, by then widowed, in Geneva in 1971 when we drove around Europe while on holidays from my job as an O&G registrar in the British National Health Service. We also met Elli in 1988 when she came to Australia for her brother Tivi's eightieth birthday but we met her daughter, my cousin Vera, only the once in 1971.

Grandma Hermin came to join us at Tessa Street, Chatswood. Shortly before she came, Dad's brother Tivi, his wife Susan and daughter Sylvia came out and stayed with us for a short while in December 1949. Children pick up languages very quickly. They spoke Slovak, not Hungarian, but they had come via Casablanca, where French was spoken. Although we can't remember a word now, in the six weeks or so they were with us, Paul and I learnt some Slovak from Sylvia and thought we were speaking French.

I remember Grandma fondly, as she was good to me. Despite her age and ill health, she would come with me into the city from Chatswood on the train and we would go up to the Australian Museum in College Street, where she would rest on a bench in the main foyer while I wandered around the museum in seventh heaven. I was a studious child rather than sports-loving, as I was no good at all with a ball. I still am not, although I now enjoy following the cricket and, having lived in Townsville for eleven years, would have no soul if I did not support the Cowboys in rugby league.

I have learnt recently from other family members that Grandma did have her issues and gave my Dad a hard time, which was hardly fair.

Grandma's health problems caught up with her and she passed away in 1953 at the age of seventy-two while we were still living in Chatswood.

Tivi was an accomplished architect and also town planner for Banska Bystrica. However, his qualifications were not recognised in Australia so he worked initially as a draftsman at the then Sydney County Council in the Queen Victoria Building, then later went back to uni and got his Australian architecture qualifications. He designed both the renovation extensions to our home at East Roseville and the conversion of the existing cottage in Lane Cove into Semper Seal's offices. Meanwhile, his wife Susan worked at Hilton's as a dress designer, also at the Queen Victoria Building. This was before the QVB was allowed to deteriorate before being renovated by a Malaysian firm into the beautiful building it is today.

Jeno and Elizabeth Partos, their daughter Susan, Susan's husband Joe Fisher and their daughter Cathy came from Israel in 1952. They had moved to Netanya in the north of Israel. Susan tells me that although it was a beautiful place, life was very hard and they had no family there, so they too decided to come to Australia. Leaving Israel was very hard for Joe, a devout Jew.

Dad's sister Lilly Elfer and her children John and Anne also came out in about 1951. John stayed with us for a while and Dad bought, or helped to buy, a unit for Lilli in Woollahra. She later moved to Cremorne. I am not totally sure whether she owned both units or rented at Woollahra and bought at Cremorne. I do know that Dad kept his promise to make sure she was looked after, although he was pretty quiet about it.

In those days, at least one day of each weekend was occupied by either visiting relatives or Continental friends or being visited by them in turn. Of course one never turned up empty-handed. My cousin Sylvia tells the story of the box of chocolates that performed this duty until somebody made a secret little mark on the box. It duly got handed over at each visit and was subsequently identified thanks to the mark when it had done the rounds. I don't think use-by dates were in vogue then.

All the ladies of the family were excellent cooks but none better than Lilli, so a visit to her was always a culinary treat. In addition, visits to her, and maybe also the Karases, both in the eastern suburbs, were marked by the purchase of small, delicate very sweet little cakes called mignons. I probably ended up eating more than my share. Fortunately at that age and in those times, I had never heard of calories or cholesterol.

On the voyage on the *Derna*, we had met a lady called Margit Kraus (no relation). She married a wealthy eastern suburbs businessman called Strauss and they were part of the group whom we visited or were visited by. They subscribed to the American magazine *Saturday Evening Post* and I used to have a wonderful time reading that at their place. Even at that young age, I was enthralled by the wonderful cover paintings Norman Rockwell did, and other articles and advertisements gave a good picture of American life of the time.

Work and Life in Australia

When Dad came to Australia, he was forty-three years old. He had been through the trauma of the war and its aftermath. He had brought his family to a strange land with a different language in a very different world, a world not without hostility, as returned Australian soldiers were trying to find their feet again as civilians at a time of shortage of jobs and housing. And strikes. And blackouts.

Those Australians who had been prisoners of war of the Japanese had been through equally harrowing experiences and all who had been to war were traumatised by it. Amidst their own traumas, memories and difficulties there was little real understanding of just what these 'bloody refos', more kindly called 'new Australians' by Labor politician Arthur Caldwell, had been through.

As far as immigration is concerned, I was a migrant child and so feel I have the right to say the following: although we brought aspects of our culture with us and much of this, for example more exotic food and not only Italian, is now very much a part of Australian everyday life, we were nevertheless expected to become Australians. As Australia had taken us in, we were only too happy to do this and did not need to forsake our previous culture to do so. ABC radio had programs to help new Australians learn to speak English. (There was no TV until it started, in Sydney first, in 1956.)

Migrant children, in order to be part of their peer group, often reject their foreign backgrounds and identify very strongly with their new homeland. (There was nothing more embarrassing than our parents speaking Hungarian in public!) Nevertheless, our parents were only too pleased to become new Australians and proud of their acceptance as citizens at our naturalisation ceremony.

'Multiculturalism' is all well and good but it should be the absorption and addition of other cultures into Australia, not an acceptance of what might at best be called foreign enclaves. As the song says, 'We are all Australian.' Or we should be.

Until he found his feet and learnt the language, Dad took what work he could find, which was sewing buttons on raincoats in a factory in Artarmon, one suburb south of Chatswood. Considering his courage, humility and willingness to learn and fit in, it was not surprising that his workmates decided he was 'a good bloke' even if he did speak funny.

They asked him his name. There is no direct English version of Imre, although it is a common enough Hungarian name. He was not alone in transliterating it from the German form, Emerich, to Emery. His workmates found that foreign-sounding name too unusual, so they said, 'That's too hard. We'll call you Jim.' The name stuck and thereafter he was unofficially 'Jim Kraus' and anything labelled with his initials proudly said 'E.J. Kraus'.

Meanwhile, Mum, who was trained and very able in dressmaking and corsetry, plied this trade from home and made a significant contribution to the income. It is as well to mention that while Mum had considerable natural ability in that field, she was a highly intelligent woman who had been robbed of the opportunity for a university education by the racist policies of the Nazi regime.

A lady called Mrs Poppy Brown, whose son Kevin was in my school, helped her with the sewing and it was often my task to walk the couple of kilometres to and from the Brown's place in Critchett Road, Chatswood, with stuff to be sewn or whatever.

I remember one of Mum's clients was a lady who was an announcer on an ABC radio program called *Kindergarten of the Air*, to which I listened. At the time, I was only a little kid and wondered how a full-size adult lady could fit into that small radio set!

I also remember that Mum had a showcase on the pedestrian overpass at Chatswood railway station in which she displayed a corset and someone broke into the showcase and stole the corset! By then she had rented a space at the back of Cordony's hairdresser on the western side of the railway in Victoria Avenue, Chatswood, as her salon.

Some time previously, Dad had obtained a German formula for a product for treating and preventing rust. As soon as he could, he went into business to manufacture it and was the first person in Australia to do anything about corrosion prevention and treatment. He was very proud that the large crane that for a very long time was in the Garden Island naval dockyard in Sydney had been treated with his product, Ferropro. (Ferropro was available until recently, made by Selleys.) Dad developed several other products in that field and was constantly experimenting. I remember the many small glass jars full of seawater with rectangular bits of sheet steel partly coated with various versions of products to compare the corrosion on treated and untreated bits.

Dad started all this in the back part of a printing shop, Berk's Printers, run by a Hungarian Jew called Berkowicz in Pine Street, Chippendale. It was just a corrugated-iron shed and very hot in summer, especially for someone who had grown up in Europe. He outgrew this and in 1955, at the same time as he bought the house at 74A Duntroon Avenue, East Roseville, he also bought a cottage at 52 Whiting Street, Artarmon, just off the Pacific Highway. The weatherboard cottage became offices and such and the large shed at the back was the factory. The factory and offices were later moved to 19 Sirius Road, Lane Cove. These new premises again utilised an existing cottage converted into offices under Tivi's design supervision and Tivi also designed the factory building adjacent.

Dad 'cooked' the Ferropro every so often, it needing to be mixed and heated according to strict conditions in a large vat. I remember helping him in the Artarmon premises in my school holidays. I would get the empty bottles, dust them and line them up in rows. Then I would fill each bottle from a rubber tube going to an outlet in the bottom of the vat, pinching the tube with my fingers to avoid spillage between bottles, especially as the Ferropro was quite corrosive, the main active ingredient being phosphoric acid.

When they were all full, I screwed on the tops, made up the cardboard cartons, put labels on the bottles and packed the bottles into the cartons. The cartons were sealed and labelled and there you go! Dad paid me £1 ($2) for a day's work. Good money then and I bought a model kit that I could not have otherwise afforded (a Jetex Hawker Hunter). The best part was working with my Dad.

Another time, somewhat earlier, while I was still in primary school and we lived in Chatswood, Dad had occasion to rent a vehicle. It was an

Austin A40 utility (we did not have a car yet) and he surprised Paul and me by meeting us as we walked home from school and giving us a lift home for the rest of the way. He was obviously so pleased to have had this little unexpected family time with his kids.

I believe Dad and I would have liked a better relationship and deep down had that. Dad kept himself to himself for the most part and like many fathers was weighed down by business. When it's your own business, you can't afford to let it go, even briefly. What all the factors influencing Dad were, I can only guess at. His wartime experiences must have been constantly in the background and probably not helped by the aspect of Australian life where the average person would thankfully have no idea of what people such as he had gone through. There was a sizeable community of ex-Hungarian Jews and I am sure that helped.

Mum's decision to become a Christian probably stressed him as well. She was not to be contradicted and if she said so, it was so. Dad appreciated the genuine warmth of the church community and their kind and accepting spirit but underneath it all I know he felt that he was Jewish.

Both he and Mum, more so Mum, had their issues that were felt by us kids. Considering what they had been through and were coping with, that is not surprising but it did influence our childhood. Although very well looked after materially, I basically had to cope on my own. Fortunately, people such as Sunday school teachers, Junior Fellowship leaders and even some of our schoolteachers provided us with good role models.

Having said all that, Dad was a lovely man. He was respected and liked by all with whom he came in contact, whether family, friends or business associates. Although the occasions were rare, when we could be together without interference in our relationship, it was very meaningful to me and, I believe, to him. The time I spent working with him bottling Ferropro is one of my most treasured memories.

The other occasion that is etched in my memory forever is that at the end of 1959 Dad had to go on a business trip to see the people running the firms which distributed his products in Melbourne, Adelaide and Brisbane. As I had just finished school, Dad decided to give me a treat and took me with him. That trip is one of my most treasured memories.

We went on a small ship from Sydney to Melbourne, by train overnight from Melbourne to Adelaide and to my delight flew from Adelaide to Brisbane and Brisbane to Sydney. The propeller-driven DC6 airliners on domestic routes at that time were not pressurised and Dad really did not enjoy that aspect of flying. My memory may be faulty here and it may well have been the more modern Vickers Viscounts on which we travelled by then.

An amusing anecdote from this trip, somewhat at Dad's expense, was his desire while in Melbourne to see the then brand-new and much publicised Myer Music Bowl. He made enquiries as to how to get to it and we duly caught the tram. However, we had no idea at which stop to get off, so Dad kept asking the conductor, with his by then good but still less than perfect English, where we should get off for the 'Myer Music *Bowel*'.

I was so impressed by that trip that when my second son, Andrew, finished school, as I had not got to spend as much time with him until then as I would have liked and as I had never been to America, I took him there, just the two of us. The pretext was to buy a light aircraft for import into and resale in Australia. We did that but quite apart from that I am so glad I reprised that bit of father–son time to mark the end of school.

Dad retired while Heather and I were in the UK, about 1970 or 1971. I am sure he was sorry not to be handing the business down to Paul or me. At one point in my studies where I had a few hiccups, I think he was a bit disappointed in a way that I did end up getting through my exams, as otherwise he would have enticed me to work with him. At one point, Paul did work as an agent for him but that didn't work out.

He sold the business but retained ownership of the premises. Unfortunately, the building burnt down and as it was underinsured he didn't realise as much as he could have. Nevertheless, his real estate investments were sufficient for him and Mum to live comfortably. At one point, he also had an agency for some Scandinavian embroidery kits (Nordiska) but I am not sure how profitable that venture was. Mum loved embroidery, so she was happy.

In the mid-1970s, Dad developed a worrying intermittent inability to move his legs. To make a long story short, this was due to prostate cancer secondaries in the bone of his sacrum (lower spine) pressing on the nerves there. In those days before PSA and other tests had come on the horizon, this was a not uncommon first symptom of prostate cancer, even though the cancer was well developed by then.

The paralysis became more severe quite quickly, indeed acutely. Dad was awaiting surgery at the Hornsby Hospital but there were some delays in theatre that day, so his operation had to wait a few hours. The surgery was to relieve the pressure on the nerves but due to the delay, it was too late and he became paraplegic.

I did not think it was possible but due to his grit and determination Dad overcame this sufficiently to walk again with the aid of two pyramid walking sticks! That's the type of man he was. He finally succumbed to the disease in August 1977, aged seventy-two.

Part Two
My Story
'Life is not meant to be easy, my child; but take courage: it can be delightful.' – George Bernard Shaw

Schooldays

I started school at Chatswood Central School at the beginning of the school year in 1949. The school is still there and looks much the same but for a high fence around it and a walkway overpass over the Pacific Highway.

In those days, blackboards were blackboards; they only became green some time later. Also in those days only some of the classrooms had blackboards on the wall and very few had those that slid up and down so there could be two layers of blackboard. For those junior years, we had a blackboard on an easel.

The teacher would write the day and date in beautiful copperplate at the top of the board each day and I clearly remember seeing '1949' written there. By then, I had picked up a little English. It was difficult at first as I knew no English, none, hardly a word, when I first started. In those less than multicultural days, some of the other kids gave me a hard time. But I lived.

We sat at small desks. If I remember right, the seats were integral and the desks were double, one boy on each side. There was a narrow bit at the top that was fixed and had a hole for an inkwell and a groove for a pen, as we wrote with pen and nib and used blotters. The top of the desk sloped down from there towards you and was hinged with space under the top for books and so on.

When I started school, I was assigned a desk together with another lad, Roger. Roger most definitely did not give me a hard time. He had a highly developed sense of fairness and a very kind nature. He also, even at that early age, played the piano very, very well. His surname is Woodward and, after winning all preliminary piano competitions in Australia, he went on to become one of the top, if not the top, concert pianists of our times. We met when we were both only six and although nowadays we don't have the opportunity to meet face-to-face too often, our friendship remains very real and very warm. He is now professor of music at the University of San Francisco.

I remember Dad used to love it when Roger played 'Black and White Rag' for him. Roger in his turn loved the smells and tastes of Mum's cooking and also to this day appreciates the encouragement Mum gave him. She recognised talent when she saw it.

Kids learn quickly and by the time I was in third class, 1951, our teacher Mrs Pennington did not know from my speech that I was not Australian-born although, believe me, it had taken a lot of work and frustration to get there. I remember in my early times at Sunday school when we sang the chorus 'When the Roll is Called Up Yonder (I'll be there)' I couldn't understand it. I thought a 'roll' was something like a Holland blind!

I can remember struggling with new words as I slowly learnt them, such as pondering the different meanings of 'thick' and 'sick' and trying to work out which was which. Also, as street signs were labelled 'St', I thought that the brand of exercise books we used, with the logo of the well-known knight on horseback killing a dragon with a lance, had the name 'Street George'. As I read as much as I could, I wondered why men were referred to as 'Mr', which in my mind I thought was pronounced as 'brrr' but with an 'm'.

Mrs Pennington was not young. Many of our teachers were elderly and had been recalled from retirement due to the shortage of teachers caused by losses during the war. That also made class sizes larger than optimal. Mrs Pennington herself had lost a son flying a Spitfire in the UK.

Australians are very sport-minded, European Jews less so. Although I am an avid cricket fan now, I initially hated the game. I could barely speak English, had no idea of what cricket was or what one was meant to be doing. Probably for these reasons, I was told to 'feel' on a hot day at the outermost edge of the playing area. I got bored silly out there on my own while the others did something or other in the middle of the ground. There was a drain there with water flowing through it, so I amused myself by watching leaves I threw in float down on the current. I vaguely heard the teacher say to the other boys, 'Oh, leave him alone.'

This obviously changed at some point, as I do remember playing cricket a little more actively at Beauchamp Park in Chatswood a little later in my primary school years. I was no good at it, though. I could only bowl underarm and even then bowled a huge percentage of wides. This is in contrast to my middle son Andrew, who played club cricket and whose action was beautiful to watch, and my brother Paul, who played both tennis and cricket.

Primary school was up to and including sixth class. Then it was time for high school, which at the time was for five years. A rude shock going from being the senior year at primary and the biggest boys in the school to the most junior and smallest ones at high school! Another difference was that in primary school you could run in the playground whereas at high school you had to walk in the quadrangle.

We were allocated to a high school according to our exam results and I was fortunate to have secured a place at North Sydney Boys' High School. It was some time after I left that I appreciated that NSBHS had given us an education at least on a par with the best private schools.

One of the main differences between primary school and high school was the class structure. In high school, one was in a different class for every subject and may well be doing a different lot of subjects to others, for example, while we all did English, some were more focused towards different levels of mathematics or science while others were more focused on the humanities, history, different languages and so on. This was in contrast to primary school, where the classmates you started with in first class were the same mob you finished with in sixth class. While we were all different personalities, this nevertheless gave us a certain cohesiveness and unity.

We were in sixth class in 1954, and in late 1983 or early 1984 I realised that it was coming on for the thirtieth anniversary of our final year of primary school. I thought this would be a good opportunity for a reunion. At that time, we were living on a few acres just out of Windsor in the Hawkesbury region of NSW, so a venue was no problem.

Roger was visiting one day, so he and I sat down together and managed to make a list of the names of our old classmates. We had contact details for some, some had contact details for others and yet others got tracked down by going through the phone book and making calls until one hit on the right person. At the end, we had quite a good roll-up and a very good time was had by all, to the extent that we did it again the next year, this time having a picnic one Saturday in the grounds of the old school.

A couple of the old teachers were able to make it to the 1984 thirty-year reunion, including Mr Fred Dadd, who had been our sixth class teacher and was much loved and respected.

The highlight of the thirty-year reunion was the cane-breaking re-enactment.

Back in 1951 in third class, we had a new boy join us. Daniel Tocatli had just migrated to Australia from Israel with his parents and older brother Reuben. He too was thrown in at the deep end as I had been a couple of years earlier, although the kids were a couple of years older, more inquisitive and didn't give him quite as hard a time, although of course he might say different were I to ask him.

Daniel knew nothing of the language, the customs or the culture. As a result, he fell foul of our aforementioned teacher Mrs Pennington, who, either out of not understanding the situation or out of frustration, decided that Daniel should get the cane. (Yes, corporal punishment was used in those days.) Nine-year-old Daniel, on the other hand, was not one to be trifled with. He grabbed the cane out of Mrs Pennington's hand and broke it into little pieces over his knee!

So, some thirty-three years later, we found a bit of bamboo and Daniel ceremonially broke it into pieces over his knee to the cheers of all and sundry!

As I said, high school was different in that we were all in different classes. I was in one class for English, another for maths, another for science. I can't really remember but I think physics and chemistry were separate classes. I liked physics and did quite well in it, although not as well at the end as I would have liked. I struggled with chemistry for some reason. In the first three years we did Latin and I also did French and German.

My Latin teacher, a fat man called Paterson whom obviously we nicknamed 'Banjo', for some reason took a set against me. As a result, I did abysmally in Latin. I think I may have scraped a pass for the Intermediate Certificate at the end of third year but was able to drop it after that. That was a pity, as I liked the stories of the myths of ancient Greece and Rome and should have enjoyed Latin. Basically I remember reading that Caesar dug ditches in Gaul.

In second year, we were in Room 24, a very dilapidated weatherboard single classroom building detached from the main school building. I sat near the back of the Latin class and there was a kid called Holmes who sat behind me. (We had individual desks in high school.) One day, Banjo was trying to teach us the Latin word '*saepissimus*'. When he said it, Holmesy directly behind me said, 'Why piss on me?' As the voice had come from my direction, Banjo just said, 'Kraus! Out!' So I spent the rest of that period outside, relishing the freedom and greatly amused.

To my surprise, I found that the very rudimentary scraps of Latin I retained actually stood me in good stead later when I did medicine, although that just added to my OCD frustration when my colleagues invariably got the word '*adnexa*' wrong. They thought the plural was '*adnexae*'. As everyone knows, that would be the case if '*adnexa*' were feminine gender singular. It is actually neuter gender plural, the singular being '*adnexum*'.

Although NSBHS was not a technical high school, in first year we did have a double period on Friday mornings, alternating between woodwork, of which I had done a little at primary school, one week and technical drawing the next. I was not very good at that but what little I learnt has been useful to me in my hobbies ever since.

The tech drawing teacher was an old chap called Gardiner, whom we naturally called 'Spade'. We would turn the bottoms of our ties inside out when we attended his class if we felt cheeky.

Spade's fetish was that to do tech drawing properly you had to use a hard pencil, the standard HB being too soft. Only a 2H would do. The story went that in a previous year, one kid who was very good at tech drawing got a very soft, 2B, pencil and, keeping it well sharpened and using a very delicate touch, did a beautiful drawing with it. Spade saw the drawing, held it up for all the class to see as an example of what all our work should look like and said, 'Now son, tell them what pencil you used to do this.'

Another old teacher was Mr Shearman, a lovely old chap we all called 'Pop' due to his age. I think he was another of those recalled from retirement due to post-war teacher shortages. As maths was not exactly my long suit, at one point Mum got me to have some extra private tuition from Pop at his home, which I did find helpful. Apart from teaching maths, Pop's great love was stocks and shares and he spent a fair amount of time telling us all about them. If only I had listened to him!

I did both French and German. As I was reasonably good at languages, Mum wanted to maximise my achievements in these subjects and as the end of high school, with the Leaving Certificate, was approaching, she got me to have some extra lessons at an institution called Linguaclub in Liverpool Street in the southern part of downtown Sydney. Unfortunately, this was counterproductive, as the lessons were on Friday afternoons, when I was tired at the end of the school week. I often had some difficulty getting there, as many buses would not stop for anyone in school uniform. We were meant to catch the 'school specials' to take us home. The trouble was I wasn't going home! Instead I was cooped up in a small cubicle with Mr Holzl, who was probably a nice guy but whose breath smelt of garlic and who tried to polish up my German. After him was a lady called 'Mademoiselle', whose breath did not smell of garlic. She tried to polish up my French and I wish it had not been the end of the day at the end of the school week and I could have shown a bit more interest. (In the French!)

For sport at NSBHS the school was divided into four houses, each with a different coloured jersey. Or should that be guernsey? I can't remember the names and colours of the other houses but I was in one called Williams. We had green jerseys. My friend Ivor was in another house with a light blue jersey. The school issued these each season.

The sports available were swimming and cricket in the summer and rugby or soccer in the winter. However, as one could not go through life without ever playing rugby – that really would not do – we all had to play rugby in first year and soccer was not an option. That upset me as I had no idea about rugby, found it a bit rough and really didn't want to play it. I actually got my hands on the ball only once all season and at that moment had brain fade and couldn't remember in which direction our team was running! Don't ask me what position I played.

After that, I played soccer in the winter. I was OK at that, usually playing inside left in the forwards, although I did at times play most other positions. I don't recall that I ever actually scored a goal but do remember kicking a fairly good goalie's kick once when I kept goal.

We played at various different fields on different weeks, Wednesday afternoons being our sports time. One of these fields was Artarmon

Reserve, which is still there. We would walk there from school, about twenty or thirty minutes walk, then walk the shorter distance to Artarmon station after the game, to catch the train home. To get to the station, we would walk through some bushland beside the playing fields and look for flattened areas of grass and used 'Frenchies' (French letters – condoms) as schoolboys will.

In the summer, I went swimming, which meant all the kids not
playing cricket were taken by the school to the public swimming pool and let loose for the rest of the school afternoon.

On one occasion, I decided to 'give it a go' and enter in the school's annual athletics carnival. I couldn't jump or run fast so I entered in the distance races, the half-mile and mile (about 800 metres and 1,600 metres). I practised running these distances, knowing that they weren't sprints, but I had no one to coach me. Mum didn't take that much interest in what I did at school that wasn't academic and even less in sport, so I actually ended up running in my black school shoes.

When the starter's gun went off in the half-mile, I started to lope along so I could last the distance and found to my horror that everyone else had taken off like scalded cats, despite the distance to run.

Similarly, I came a distant last in the mile, to the jeers and catcalls of the kids in the stands. For once, this didn't get to me. I thought, 'They can sling off, but I'm having a go while they're not.'

I started high school while we still lived at Chatswood. I would walk the ten minutes or so to the station, cross the overpass, catch a tram and get off at the intersection of Miller and Falcon streets, where the school is. The trams stopped running soon after we moved from Chatswood. When we moved to East Roseville in 1955, when I was in first year at NSBHS, instead of a tram we lived on a bus route so I caught the 206 or 207 bus going to the city and got off at the same intersection, the bus travelling along Miller Street, while the tram had gone along Falcon Street.

At that time, the fare for schoolkids was a penny. There were twelve pence to a shilling and twenty shillings to a pound. When we went to decimal currency on 14 February 1966, a shilling became ten cents and ten shillings became the dollar. The English had the same currency system but stuck to tradition and could not let the pound go, so they retained the pound when they went decimal so their 'new pence' were like 2 cents to us.

The penny fare soon gave way to a more expensive fare of sixpence (five cents) each way. This meant that my parents had to spend five shillings a week on my fares. However, train travel for schoolkids was free. You had to apply for a little metal pass that cost nothing and took the place of a ticket going to and from school.

At East Roseville, we were on the bus route and about a mile, fifteen minutes walk, from Roseville station. The kids who caught the train to school got off at St Leonards, ten minutes walk from the school. So, with an eye to greed, I got Dad to drop me off at Roseville station on his way to work in the morning, caught the train and walked to school from St Leonards. In the afternoon, together with many other kids, I walked to St Leonards station, got off at Roseville and walked the fifteen minutes home. I retained the five bob, thus more than doubling my weekly pocket money.

My schooldays spanned the 1950s, high school being 1955 to 1959. So my teenage years were spent in the second half of the 1950s, the time of the birth of rock 'n' roll and of television in this country. I was a quiet and shy kid who mostly kept himself to himself. It was great to sit by the radio in my own world in my room listening to the hit parades, especially on Saturday night. I remember the new era ushered in by Bill Haley and the Comets with 'Rock Around the Clock'.

It was the era of the likes of Buddy Holly, the Big Bopper, the Platters, the Everly Brothers and Johnny Cash, not to mention Elvis, Johnny Mathis, Johnny Ray, Guy Mitchell and so on, and fun novelty numbers like 'My Friend the Witch Doctor', 'Seven Little Girls (Sitting in the Back Seat)', 'The Flying Purple People Eater' and some fun English ones like Lonnie Donegan's 'Does Your Chewing Gum Lose Its Flavour on the Bed Post Overnight' 'What a Mouth' and 'My old Man's a Dustman'. (All still classics and available on Youtube to this day.) Every day seemed to bring new hits that I knew even then would remain all-time classics. What an era in which to be a teenager!

For publicity, Elvis's colour was purple, 'Presley Purple', and Guy Mitchell's a bright turquoise, 'Mitchell Blue'. If you wanted to be a real lair, you wore socks of those colours. But not to school, not if you wanted to live.

TV started in Sydney in 1956. We sat on our school cases waiting for the bus home and could see the TV transmission towers going up, one stage at a time.

Channel 9 was the tallest tower, then Channel 7 and, slightly smaller, ABC Channel 2. Channel 10 only came along later, in the 1960s, to much denigration and jeering from the other stations and often amateurish beginnings, like shaky sets.

At first, only the privileged few, or those with very turned-on parents, had TV sets, so we would go to the lucky others' places and watch favourite shows like *77 Sunset Strip*, *Rawhide* (which introduced Clint Eastwood), *Maverick* and many others including the ever popular *Bandstand*, hosted by Brian Henderson, who went on to a long career with Channel 9. *Bandstand* featured artists such as Col Joye and the Joye Boys, Frank Ifield, Johnny O'Keefe, the Delltones (from 1958) and others. Crowds would also gather out of hours at the windows of electrical and department stores to watch programs of public interest on TV sets on display there.

TV sets broadcast in black and white, although the tonal quality wasn't always good. They weren't properly rectangular but the sides were convexly curved. The common size was seventeen inches but if you were rich or ostentatious you got a twenty-one-inch set. Until digital TV came along fairly recently, the picture was actually made up of horizontal lines. There was the same number of lines whether the screen was large or small, so you had to sit further back from the larger sets.

It is interesting that despite us using metric measurements for a long time now, TV sets today still advertise their size in inches. The other relic of pre-decimal days is the weight of babies. We have weighed babies in grams or kilograms for the last fifty years but when I was delivering them, everyone wanted to know the weight in pounds. I was always amused when a young woman who would have no idea of what half a pound of butter would be claimed she didn't know how big a baby was if the weight was expressed as three kilograms instead of six pounds five ounces.

Many of the TV shows were half an hour long with an ad break of three thirty-second ads at the quarter-hour mark and between shows. And we complained then about too many ads!

Hobbies

Apart from God, my wife, family and dog, the two great loves of my life are aircraft and photography. These started to develop quite early.

I can remember making my first model aircraft while we still lived at Chatswood, so I would have been around eleven or twelve. You could buy kits for what we called 'solid models' in a scale similar to the plastic models we make today, which replaced them.

These would consist of a small box with a plan, a balsa block the right size for the fuselage and some sheet balsa with the outlines of the wings and tail printed on it. You traced the outline of the fuselage from the plan onto the balsa block and carved and sanded it to shape. You then cut out the wings and tail from the sheet, sanded them smooth and stuck them on with balsa cement. They could then be painted with dope and then coloured paint.

You could also buy flying model kits, rubber-powered and cut out from very flimsy one-sixteenth-inch (1.5mm) balsa assembled with mainly one-sixteenth-inch-square balsa strip. All the parts had to be cut out of the sheet and the whole thing was so flimsy I don't remember if I ever actually finished one. They were meant to be powered by winding up a long rubber band which then unwound to turn the propeller.

When I was fourteen, I actually got, after much harassment of my parents, a second-hand model aircraft engine! It was an ED brand 1.46cc Hornet and cost £3. It was actually quite a good example and I am annoyed with myself that I ever sold it. I did so when I got old enough to drive, and cars displaced model aircraft. I did not realise that aeromodelling and aircraft are in your DNA and you can never get them out of your system. Today I have a quite significant collection of the old model engines, mainly the ED brand. This includes several examples of the 1.46cc Hornet, but I wish I had kept that first one.

My uncle Tivi *bacsi*, though, was more supportive and bought me a set of X-Acto modelling knives in a little wooden box for my fourteenth birthday. I suspect he may have hoped I might build him models of the houses he designed but that would have been asking too much and he never said so. I really appreciated that gift, which acknowledged my interest, and I still have the little wooden case in which the knives came.

My mother was more supportive of my photography, I think because she had been very fond of the younger of her two older brothers, Andor, Bandi for short, who had been lost in the Holocaust. Bandi *baci* had been interested in photography. Indeed, the camera the family had, and which I still have, was a Voigtlander which had originally belonged to him. However, at the time it was the only camera the family had and Mum was the one who used it. The viewfinder did not have any correction for parallax so she invariably cut off people's heads in photos, a well-known hazard of cameras of the day.

As she wished to encourage me in photography, when I was twelve or thirteen, she bought me for Christmas or birthday a box camera. Typically, when everyone else had a Kodak Box Brownie, she bought me a similar camera of the German Agfa brand. It took eight photos on 120 film. The Box Brownie used 620 film, which was the same film but used a slightly different spool.

In those days, the film, black and white of course, was what they called orthochromatic. Shortly thereafter, panchromatic film, sensitive to all colours of light although still black and white, arrived on the scene. The panchromatic film gave better tones but the earlier film was a tad less fussy in the developing process.

Being a poor but independent little lad, instead of paying to have it developed I learnt from books how to do it yourself. It was very simple. You bought developer and fixer, obtainable from the local chemist ,who also sold film and was an agent where you could leave films for processing and pick the photos up next week. You then borrowed three small glass dishes from Mum and put developer in one, water in the second and fixer in the third. Then at night, with the room dark and the family warned not to open the door, you unrolled the exposed film and, holding it at each end so it hung down between your hands, you dunked it in the developer, lifting each end alternately so as to run the entire length of film through the developer, keeping it moving so the developer worked on the whole film. After doing this for the time stated on the instructions, you then washed it in a similar manner in the next little dish of water, then in the fixer.

After the fixing was done, you could turn the lights back on and take the film to the bathroom or laundry, where it got put under running water for the appointed time then hung up with a peg to dry. I later got a developing tank which made life easier. That gave you negatives.

To print them, I bought a simple 'contact frame'. This was like a small picture frame, six by nine centimetres – that is, the size of each negative on the film. You put the negative into this and, in the dark or with a safelight for illumination, put a sheet of sensitised photo paper behind it and put the back on the frame. This was then exposed to light for a few seconds, carefully timed, then the light was turned off and the paper developed and fixed in the same solutions as for the film. This resulted in a contact print, a black and white print six by nine centimetres, the same size as the negative, and if you did it right, the same as you got back from the chemist in those early days. It was only much later that I was able to buy an enlarger.

It is remarkable how one's eyes become adapted to the dark. Shapes slowly materialise out of the gloom until you can see almost well enough to read a newspaper, even without the safelight on. Not only does the eye have an iris diaphragm like a camera, but the retina becomes more or less sensitive to light depending on the conditions, just like a photographer can use a slower or faster film for different light conditions. Digital cameras have this same facility. I cannot understand atheists who seem to think that such complex and sophisticated mechanisms just accidentally made themselves by chance.

When I was sixteen, at the end of fourth year in high school, I had my first job, helping out with the Christmas rush at the post office. I bought a better camera with that first pay packet. I wish I could remember what I eventually did with it.

The family had driven up for our first trip to the Gold Coast and as I had the post office job, I followed a little later. That was my first ever time in an aeroplane, a Vickers Viscount. Then on the Gold Coast I had just enough money left over after buying the camera to go on my first light aircraft flight, a joy flight in the back seat of an Auster. I still have the photo I developed and printed which I took with my new camera during my first light aircraft flight. Who could ask for anything more in life?

On a more sombre note, we stayed at a motel there in Southport and there was a great commotion one day in the motel across the road. Apparently a little girl of three years old had fallen into the pool and drowned. Something to remember when one feels that today's laws about swimming pools are a restrictive nuisance.

When I look at pictures I took way back in my teens in the early days, I am surprised at what I was able to achieve with such simple equipment. I am distressed, though, when I see the photos I took in my twenties and thirties that the work I did then seems to me to be better than what I do now. I must be past my peak, although in recent years I have had some aviation photojournalism published, including a cover photo on a former American international aviation magazine.

I turned seventeen when I was in my last year of high school. You had to be seventeen to get your driver's licence but you could get your learner's permit at sixteen years and ten months. (There were no P plates then.) I was taught to drive by Mr Kavanagh, who had a black Morris Minor, an old 'low light' one, fitted with dual controls. It felt great to be in the driver's seat and actually controlling the car.

On the appointed day, I took myself off for my driving test, passed it and went into town and saw the movie *South Pacific*. Mum was beside herself by the time I got home and asked why I hadn't rung her. I told her that she knew I was going to see the movie after the driving test so what was she on about. There were no mobile phones in those days but I could have used a public phone. She said I could have let her know whether I had passed the test or not, to which I replied that of course I had passed, what did she expect, so why should I call? Such is youth!

For the record, not only were there no mobile phones, there were also no flashing turn indicators on cars, so one signalled one's intentions with hand signals. For that, the driver's window had to be open but, as there was no air conditioning either, that didn't matter so much. Except perhaps when it rained hard. A heater was an optional extra on some of the better cars.

My First Car

At high school, I was quite good friends with a boy called Bob Brierly, with whom I am still in contact. Bob's older brother Phil was a motor mechanic and if I remember right was rebuilding a historic Model A Ford. Bob and Phil introduced me to Singer cars, particularly the Singer 9.

Of course secretly most of us wanted an MG but the Singer was more affordable. It was a two-door convertible but unlike the MG had a rear seat, which was useful. And a boot. Frankly it was also more comfortable than the MG. It had a single overhead cam (!) engine of 1074cc developing, if I remember right, all of thirty-seven horsepower. Although the earlier versions had a three-speed gearbox, my 1951 model had a four-speed manual box. You could loosen a couple of wing nuts at the sides of the windshield frame and fold the windscreen down flat. Phil had the slightly later version with a 1.5-litre motor. Wow!

My parents had regularly put a small amount of money aside into an account for me and gave it to me when I finished school. It amounted to about £100. The average going rate for a Singer 9 was £95.

The Singer was great fun to drive, as it oversteered considerably. There is now a suburb of Sydney right by East Roseville called Castlecove. At that time, though, it was just a new housing development by the L.J. Hooker people, which they called Castle Heights Estate. It was made streets but as yet no houses or people, so I enjoyed taking the Singer down there, taking the corners fast, flicking the tail out and doing a four-wheel slide round the corner. That's when you use 'opposite lock'.

Like all cars of its day, the Singer had a separate chassis with a body bolted onto it. What was less common was that the body was aluminium panels on a wooden frame. One of the car's less endearing qualities was that it would regularly break the rear axle half shaft where the splined bit went into the differential. I became quite adept at jacking the back of the car up and replacing the half shaft. The problem really was that when one side broke, it put a strain on the other side, which weakened it so in the fullness of time it too would break, and so it went on. The answer should have been to replace both sides with intact parts but as I could only ever afford one second-hand half shaft at a time from the wreckers…

After a while, my Singer developed just a few too many problems. The Brierlys were friends with a chap in the western suburbs, Gavin O'Shea, who was very much into Singers and a bit of an unofficial club leader for those younger ones of us who were like-minded. Gavin traded my car on another Singer 9. This was a slightly later model with independent front suspension but otherwise similar. I pulled the engine of this car apart and replaced the rings and bearings. I don't think it really needed it but 'doing rings and bearings' was a kind of rite of passage for anyone into cars in those days. Phil Brierly's advice and some help were invaluable.

Camp Bevington

In my later years at high school, Mum sent me, and following in due course also my brother Paul, to a summer camp, Camp Bevington, run by ISCF, a Christian organisation. At any rate, they taught us good Christian principles there.

The commandant was a man called Phil Caiger, a pharmacist in real life who gave up his holiday time to lead our camp. His deputy was Bill Winser, a younger man a few years my senior whom I knew as he was leader of Junior Fellowship at our church, St Barnabas Roseville East, and, as I discovered later, was also big in the Evangelical Union (EU) at Sydney University. I also knew a couple of the other camp leaders, David Loader and Bob Mirrington, from our church's Junior Fellowship.

David went on to become a teacher and became the first and possibly only male headmaster of an exclusive girls' private school. At that time, however, he also made a little money for himself making rope doormats by twisting rope on a wooden frame. He subcontracted some to me, which helped my pocket money situation.

Bob was brilliant at organic chemistry. A short while later, when I was in my first year at university, I would visit him in the lab in the beautiful new chemistry building where Bob was doing his research and pass the time with him. We later renewed our friendship as Bob had become ordained into the Anglican Church and became rector of the small parish at Pitt Town, close to where we lived at the time.

Camp Bevington was on the shores of Lake Munmorah, on the central coast a little north of Sydney. There were wooden platform floors above which tents sleeping several of us had been erected for our accommodation. We ate and had meetings in a larger marquee.

Camp Bevington was a sailing camp. As well as Christian songs, we sang sea shanties and had a rollicking good time. The sailing was in, or really on, small boats called Vaucluse Juniors, VJs for short. This was a class devised for racing in one of Sydney's sailing clubs.

The boats we had were discards from racing, mainly as they had become too heavy, and they did vary quite a bit from one to the other in their performance. They were sloop-rigged and had a crew of two, the skipper, who sat aft and handled the mainsheet and tiller, and the for'ard hand, who handled the jib. They had a closed deck you sat on top of with a well in the middle to put your feet into and a centreboard keel. The performance variations in the boats really didn't matter. We were kids being taught to sail and having fun boat rides. We didn't hold any races.

As a kid, I was a bit of a loner and an avid reader. When we lived in Chatswood, I was a regular at the public library. I knew all about the adventures of Budge and Betty, who had a magic ring that would turn toys into the real thing. I knew all about Dr Doolittle and his ability to talk to the animals, his adventures flying to the moon on the back of the giant moth, the hairs of which trapped enough air to breathe while travelling through space, and the push-me-pull-you, a llama with two front parts that met in the middle. (I wondered about that: two ends that ate and no end that…)

I had learnt to fly by reading Biggles and had learnt to sail reading the Swallows and Amazons books by Arthur Ransome set in the Lakes District of England. I really had learnt to sail reading those books. When Bill Winser took me out on a VJ on Lake Munmorah, he just couldn't believe I had never sailed before. I knew what a sheet was and how to handle it to set the sail, I knew what a tack, a reach and running before the wind were, also going about and jibing and what you did to perform these manoeuvres.

I had read in one of the kids' adventure books that if you were being looked for and you stayed still, perfectly still, you would be very hard to spot. One night we had a game where half of us, on one team, were taken to the top of the hill overlooking the camp and had to make our way through the fairly open bush down to the camp without being spotted by the remaining kids who were the other team. If you were caught, you were out.

I was in the team trying to get down the hill and back to camp. I heard a group of kids on the other team very close and knew they would catch me so I crouched down by a tuft of long grass and didn't move a muscle. Those kids were standing literally right next to me, discussing tactics and where they could look for or find us and it was several minutes before one of them happened to glance down and see me at their feet. I nearly got away with it.

Paul and I had small suitcases for our luggage but a lot of the kids had old army kitbags, probably left over from their fathers' war service or bought at army surplus stores. These were long sausage-shaped canvas bags closed at one end with a drawstring at the other and very good for such a camp.

Going home at the end of the camp, we caught a train from Gosford. Our carriage happened to be one of those beautiful old ones, an antique even back then. Varnished wooden slats for seats and luggage racks and a beautiful cylindrical glass bottle with a spigot, with water for the passengers to drink. One of the kids, a big and rather larger than life fellow, eyed off this very attractive water container, looked at its diameter and the diameter of his kit bag and said, 'Pity. It won't fit.' He was serious.

I was appalled. Here we were having just spent time at a Christian camp, being taught not only to sail but also very good moral principles for life, and on the way home he wanted to steal. That taught me a bit about human nature, though.

University

Like many others, even in late high school I had no idea what I wanted to do for a career. My parents, having had the ability but having been deprived of the opportunity to go to university, were insistent that I should go to uni but were not at all directive about what I should do there.

Then, near the end of my school time, I read a couple of books by Jurgen Thorwald, *Century of the Surgeon* and *Triumph of Surgery*. I still have them. They are narrated in the first person by a fictitious doctor who made it his business to travel around the world to observe first hand advances in the medical field, especially surgery, and report on them. I thought that seemed as good a career as any so I enrolled in Medicine at the University of Sydney.

In those days, the exam at the end of school was called the Leaving Certificate. You had to do six subjects and pass in four to gain the certificate. The levels of pass were Honours, A and B. To do Honours, you had to nominate beforehand to do it and it was a separate exam. The Honours paper was only marked if you scored an A in the basic exam.

I sat for English, French (in which I nominated for Honours) maths I, maths II, physics and chemistry. I scored As in English and French and Bs in the other four subjects. I was disappointed not to have done better in physics. I missed out on Honours in French, as I knew I would. The Honours paper was well after the other tests were finished and, try as I might, I just couldn't settle down and concentrate to study by then.

When I sat the English paper, I knew I had done well and was sorry I had not nominated for Honours, which I probably would have got. I had been in the B class for English. This was no shame; the A class was for those kids who were much more into the humanities, History and such and that wasn't my thing. A lot of us in the B class did well, but at our level and with our approach. All the same I felt, and still feel, I could have passed the Honours exam but by the time I realised that, it was too late to nominate.

Entrance to university in those days was quite different to what it became not that much later. You could go to university provided you matriculated in your Leaving exam. Matriculation required passes in five subjects, not four, one of which had to be English. There were university fees that were paid at the time, not the stressful incurring of debt as happens today with HECS fees. However, if you did well enough in the Leaving Certificate, or passed your annual university exams, you could get a Commonwealth scholarship, which paid the fees.

I did not do quite well enough in the Leaving to get such a scholarship, so Dad paid my first year fees, then I got the scholarship when I passed at the end of the year.

Apart from the matriculation requirement, there were no restrictions on entry into any faculty, thus everybody was given an opportunity. I lost count of the number of older adults I met who, on asking what I did and being told I was a medical student, said, 'I was a medical student once.'

Most people did arts, gaining a bachelor's degree, BA, or science, BSc. There were of course other faculties such as vet science, dentistry, architecture, pharmacy, engineering, law, physiotherapy and so on. Nursing was not a university degree at that time.

There was meant to be a tradition of hostility between engineering and medicine, like the feeling between Sydney and Melbourne, but I never saw it. We had the feeling that a lot of the girls doing arts were just doing it for the sake of getting some letters after their name and marking time until they found a husband. Not a very politically correct thought today and, although I am sure there may have been some truth in that, I don't think there was much.

Medicine was a six-year undergraduate course. The challenge was not to get into medicine but to stay in it. There was a high failure rate. A university song went, 'The Profs have issued a new decree, that 50% must fail, must fail.'

Indeed, the failure rate in first year was fifty per cent, as it was in second year. In third year it dropped to twenty per cent but by then it was a pretty select population. Few failed after that but some did repeat final year. In the old days, there were horror stories of people taking twelve years to do the six-year course but this was stopped by the time we were on the scene. The rule was that you could not repeat any year more than once and had three years to get through the first two. About eighty per cent of the students repeated a year somewhere along the way. Medicine was acknowledged as being the toughest of all the courses and a single moment's inattention at any time could spell disaster for that year.

All that is in contrast to what followed when the kids had to do well enough in the HSC to get into the faculty of their choice. This meant that people were virtually railroaded into medicine, law or vet science not because that was their passion but so as not to miss the opportunity their good pass opened for them. Then, having been accepted into the bottom end of their training, they were assured of being spat out the top end in due course. In contrast to when I went through, it became hard to get into medicine and easy to stay in it.

To my mind, this created people who may or may not have been the right type of people to be doctors but who thought they were God's gift to mankind as they had done well enough to do medicine. It also favoured the girls, as they mature more quickly than boys and it takes that maturity to apply oneself sufficiently to get those good grades at the end of school.

Others must have had similar thoughts, as many universities now require interviews for potential medical students as well as requiring a reasonable minimum academic standard. I was privileged to sit on one of those committees for a while at Townsville's James Cook University. The committee included people from several different fields, including a lay representative.

The first three years were the 'preclinical' years when we learnt basic sciences such as anatomy, physiology and biochemistry. This was all completed by the end of third year and third year only took the first two of the three university terms. The third term of third year was called junior fourth year and prepared us for the clinical years when we saw live patients. In junior fourth year, we were introduced to things such as pathology, histology, pharmacology and so on. Fourth year continued these and introduced medicine and surgery, and briefly touched on medical jurisprudence. Psychiatry and paediatrics were also in there somewhere. Fifth year added obstetrics and gynaecology and was half a day at uni and the second half at our teaching hospital.

We started to go to our allotted teaching hospitals in fourth year and by final year hardly ever went to the university campus. Medical students in hospital wore short white coats, junior residents (now interns) wore white trousers and short white coats and registrars wore street clothes under a long white coat.

For someone such as myself, who had done physics and chemistry at school, first year was a doddle. It was more challenging for those whose high schooling was more into the humanities. We did physics, chemistry, zoology and an elective subject, for which I chose a year of psychology. Physics and chemistry were little more than a revision of what I had done for the leaving, although chemistry became organic chemistry in third term and that wasn't so easy for me.

We had lectures in the various different venues at the university and the practical zoology class was in the zoology building. It was a double session and lasted all morning, or afternoon, I forget which. My memories are of the overwhelming smell of formalin on entering the building. Fortunately, the sense of smell adapts fairly quickly.

We dissected frogs and dogfish, among others. The lecturer of zoology was a gentle man by the name of Colefax. As soon as he opened his mouth to talk to us, many of us recognised his voice as that of 'Tom the Naturalist' of *The Argonauts*, an ABC radio program for older children. We could buy preserved dogfish to take home and dissect at leisure.

I have never been overconfident in exams or considered myself particularly brilliant academically but looking around at my cohort of first year students I could not get worried by the fifty per cent failure rate awaiting us at year's end. All were really nice people whose hearts and personalities were right but it was quite obvious that they just didn't have what it was going to take to stay the course. At least they had the chance and could say they tried.

Second year was a different kettle of fish. Medicine was acknowledged as the hardest course at university and second year was acknowledged as the hardest year.

I disciplined myself to a strict study timetable. I arrived home late afternoon from uni and relaxed or helped Mum for the short time until dinner. Dinner was over by seven p.m. and I had a strict study timetable from then until one a.m.: revise each lecture from that day, then study the various subjects in one-hour blocks, with a five-minute break between hours and a half-hour 'quiet time' to pray and read God's word. Then it was off to bed for six hours sleep and up at seven the next morning. Without that regimen, I could not have made it.

What we awaited with both great anticipation and dread as we entered second year was anatomy. We were assigned in groups to dissect cadavers, embalmed corpses. These were bodies that had been left to the university by those people one meets who say they are 'leaving their bodies to science'. As such, we were taught to treat them with due respect and no one had any problem with that. This was in contrast to doctors a generation older than us. They dissected cadavers of people whose bodies were unclaimed, or who were unidentified derelicts who had died in the gutter or a park. Unfortunately, some of the stories indicated that they had not been required to treat the cadavers respectfully.

We dissected on stainless steel tables like those seen regularly on TV shows depicting autopsy (post-mortem) scenes. Each cadaver was dissected by two teams, one dissecting head, neck and upper limbs and the other the thorax, abdomen, pelvis and lower limbs. Halfway through the year, we got new cadavers and changed over.

The dissecting room was also a social meeting place where one sat and discussed the important things of life, especially religion, politics and so on. One incident there unfortunately remains in my memory.

Another student whom I knew to speak to as his surname also began with K came up to me and made a derogatory comment about the numbers of Asian students. We had quite a few who were studying under the Colombo Plan. I couldn't quite understand his meaning so I said, 'What?' and he repeated it. I was appalled that there were people among my own peer group who overtly felt that way but I guess I was naive. That opened my eyes a bit. I have been saddened but less surprised when in later years people of whom I would have thought better expressed similar sentiments. As I said earlier, they are in every society.

For some time now, students do not dissect. They learn their anatomy from specimens dissected by expert prosectors to display the various items of anatomy being studied.

The other thing needed for anatomy was a skeleton. A half skeleton really – that is, skull, spinal column with one side of the pelvis and the arm, leg and ribs from one side. These could be bought from the medical supply houses but most were passed on second-hand from one generation of students to the next. They were stored in a wooden crate that we naturally referred to as a coffin and most of us stored under our beds at home. The bones were not articulated – that is, they were separate. I think they may have been sourced from India. Certainly the one I had was of small stature although obviously a mature adult. Most politically incorrect today and really not quite ethically or morally right when you come to think about it, but that was what we did and accepted then.

Third year was much the same as second year except that I allowed myself to be distracted and failed my old nemesis, biochemistry. I didn't do too badly, though, and was therefore eligible to do a 'post', which was a second chance exam, but didn't make it.

In the Real World

Disappointing though failing third year may have been at the time, it was actually the best thing that could have happened. This was third year I failed, so my university year in 1962 ended at the end of second term. That left me with about six months before I had to start back for a second go at third year. I had worked Saturday mornings and uni holidays at a camera store in town, which is where this narrative started. I was able to work full-time for those six months. Thus I was able to support myself financially and, more importantly, experience the real world for a while.

The camera store was in George Street, on the western side, between Market and King streets. It was just up the road from the Kodak headquarters, which were on the corner of George and King. There is still a narrow little lane beside that building which opens out into a small yard. The shop, called Magnetic Sound, had a Morris Minor panel van it kept there. At times, I had to run messages for the shop using that van, so I got used to driving in the congested city traffic, but most of all the challenge was to get that little van in and out of the tiny space at the top of the lane. That required a good deal of backing and filling.

Magnetic Sound was owned by Noel Gay. His younger brother Russell also worked there. Noel Gay lived not far from us in East Roseville and occasionally gave me a lift home after work.

The pay and conditions were not brilliant but I guess they were about the norm for the times. Every so often, we rearranged the window display. This was done after hours but we were not paid any overtime; it was considered to be just part of the job. We did get a meal at a Chinese restaurant afterwards, though. I think my regular pay was a little over £7 per week plus a small bonus for any sales over £50 in one day.

Saturday mornings were the busiest. In those days, shops were only open half day on Saturday and closed Sunday. On a typical Saturday morning, we would do as much business as on a regular weekday.

One day I was at the counter and a very glamorous, heavily made-up young woman wearing very high heels and tight leopard skin patterned slacks came in with a film to be developed. I got the envelope into which we put films and, starting to fill out the top portion, asked her name. She appeared somewhat miffed that I had to ask her but gave it to me; I duly filled out the details and gave her the stub.

Russell Gay had been watching this with some amusement and said to me, 'Do you know who that was?' I knew as she had given me her name. It was Lana Cantrell, the well-known singer.

As the name implies, Magnetic Sound was basically a tape recorder store and tape recorders were Mr Gay's passion. The camera department was downstairs. When in Sydney recently, I found that there was a Ted's Camera Store on that site so I went downstairs to look at their cameras and have a chat. Ted Todd, who started Ted's Cameras, was a sales rep for one of the wholesale companies when I worked in the trade. He was a Hungarian like me and a nice guy, so we got on well. He started his own business that became a chain, which he has long since sold. In those days, he had Saturday mornings free and occasionally moonlighted, right there where again there was a camera store, now bearing his name.

The camera department downstairs at Magnetic Sound had three salesmen apart from myself. The head salesman was a Czech Jew called Frank Klein. The other two were a chap called Fred Godin and a Belgian guy called Henry, but I can't remember his surname. We all got on well. Frank took me under his wing and taught me how to sell to such good effect that I, the newbie, outsold the two older and more experienced salesmen. That helped the pocket with the small bonuses earnt.

Frank's rules were simple:
1. Know your stock.
2. Find out what your customer wants.
3. Check on the customer's budget.

The late great motivational speaker and salesman, Zig Ziglar, said that a good salesman was not one who could sell fridges to Eskimos. That was a con man. A good salesperson was one whose motivation was that their client should be better off if they bought the product. That's really what Frank taught me. Make sure that customer leaves the shop with a product that will do the job they want done at a price they can afford or, at the very least, a compromise with which they are happy.

It's also the principle I later taught my students and trainee doctors with regard to handling patients who were reluctant to accept treatment that would benefit them.

Frank was a bit of a character. He drove a 1951 Bentley, which according to his descriptions of his driving, he drove as if it were a Formula 1 car, and he probably did. Both he and Henry had been professional photographers in their day and enjoyed a friendly rivalry, Frank having always used a Speed Graphic camera and Henry some other that I can't remember. Frank told numerous anecdotes ending with '...but of course I can't now. I'm married.'

Frank earned himself the nickname 'Cranky Frankie' as he would yell and shout and pretend to be most impatient to people he rang up on business. I was told off most properly by an elderly gentleman at Kodak when I tried to emulate Frank and learned my lesson.

Frank was offered a job managing another camera store, Globe Cameras, on the other side of George Street just north of the Liverpool Street corner. I went with him and we had a very good time in a friendly, relaxed and profitable environment. After I went back to uni, I continued to work there on Saturdays and uni holidays, up to when I had already sat and passed my final exams but before I started work as a junior resident doctor. Frank loved telling everyone I served in the shop that I was a doctor. He was like a proud father.

Back to University and the Teaching Hospitals

When the time was up, it was back to uni to do third year again and proceed from there. This time, I applied myself and regained the Commonwealth scholarship for junior fourth year.

During that year my aunt by marriage, Mum's late brother Leslie's widow, Marti *neni*, came to Australia for a visit. I had not seen her since I was six and would not see her again until I visited Budapest for the first time in 2000, thirty-eight years later.

I had applied for and was accepted for a student placement at the Royal North Shore Hospital.

In fourth year, we spent our mornings at university, now in the new Medical School on the other side of the university oval to the main university campus and the Anderson Stuart building, the old Medical School, where we had spent second and third years.

Fourth year at the teaching hospitals was when they taught us to examine patients. Public patients were treated for free. In those pre- Medicare days, there was a means test to be a public patient and the consultants were called 'honoraries' because they saw the public patients, and gave their time to teach us, free.

In return for the free treatment, maybe with the help of the junior medical staff but nevertheless at the same standard of care as private patients, the public patients were meant to make themselves available to us to take their histories and examine them. Although this was the arrangement, we were always required to ask and did so but only occasionally got a refusal.

We were organised into student groups and had a tutor for medicine and one for surgery. During tutorials, we were told how to examine patients and given the experience of doing so under supervision as well as being let loose to practise on our own.

Our surgical tutor was Mr Noel 'Chook' Fowler and for medicine we had Dr Ian Thomas. They were both great people, Dr Thomas a little more restrained in his personality than Chook Fowler but competent, sympathetic and not without a sense of humour. A good teacher.

Likewise, Chook was very good to us. A confirmed bachelor well into middle age, he taught us well. Surgeons are or were called 'Mr' as a form of reverse snobbery. The origins of surgery lie with the old barber surgeons who were not doctors, hence the traditional red and white striped barbers' poles. These days, in our more relaxed and less traditional environment, even surgeons tend to be called 'Doctor' in most places.

My father couldn't understand what we were taught in surgery. He wanted to know if they taught us where to cut. That's operative surgery. What our surgical training was about was dealing with surgical conditions, for example how to recognise the history, signs and symptoms of, say, appendicitis and what needed to be done about it.

North Shore Hospital at that stage was in older premises. The first stages of the new ones, casualty and operating theatres, were starting to be built when we were students and completed just as we were finishing. The old operating theatres had a viewing gallery where, from a vantage point and behind a glass window, you could see surgery proceeding. It was mainly for show, really, and satisfied our lust to see blood and gore. To properly see an operation, you have to be in close, as when scrubbed up and assisting.

I remember an exception to that when I watched an orthopaedic surgeon do a knee arthrodesis. Knee replacements were a long way off yet and, orthopaedics at that stage being little more than glorified carpentry, was simple in principle. Basically, the surgeon cut the knee joint out and fixed the end of the tibia to the end of the femur, at an angle of about fifteen degrees. While crude, this gave the patient relieffrom the pain of his arthritis and a leg with which he could still sit, stand and walk, after a fashion.

It's a pity I didn't do orthopaedics. I would be richer and less burnt-out now if I had. What stopped me was seeing adolescents with severe chronic spinal conditions who had to lie unmoving in a plaster bed for six months. If anyone had done that to me, I would be a screaming nervous wreck and felt I couldn't do it to anyone, even if it was to his or her ultimate benefit.

I'm not sure I ever saw that again after my student days, so maybe I should have done orthopaedics and had a much easier life.

Royal North Shore was home to a pioneering unit for spinal injuries run by the great Dr John Yeo. When we lived in, we were challenged to a wheelchair basketball match by the paraplegics, who beat us soundly!

Fifth year added obstetrics and gynaecology, and anaesthetics also fitted in somewhere. We lived in for a short time in turns during our obstetrics training, as we had to be on hand to do our required number of deliveries. We were housed in a rather dilapidated hut, several at a time, and we got up to some high jinks there while waiting for women to have their babies.

Most people don't know where the term 'obstetrics' comes from. The 'stet' is the same as the typist's term which means 'let it stand'. The obstetrician is meant to stand by while the woman delivers her baby. This is a good principle to remember but it is as well that there is an obstetrician, or midwife, as most people, correctly saying that having babies is 'natural,' forget that having babies safely is not and do not realise that without proper care, the maternal mortality rate – yes, women dying in childbirth – is between sixty and a hundred per thousand – that is, six to ten per cent. This sad figure applies to undeveloped countries to this day and is in stark contrast to today's high expectations. These expectations come thanks to a lot of effort, although most regular antenatal care, while important, is not stressful.

The most frustrating times in my career were when I achieved a healthy mother and healthy baby in a situation where just the opposite was likely without intervention yet the mother was disappointed and angry, with permanent negative feelings about her childbirth, due to things being different to what she had wanted and planned. I have even been told off good and proper by a husband because I was upfront with a lady who clearly was going to need a Caesarean but who wanted a natural birth.

Our obstetrics and gynaecology tutor was Mr David Pfanner, who was a bit of a character and not backward in coming forward. The story goes that while attending one birth something happened and he found the midwife was inadvertently getting in the way between him and the patient, so he yelled at her, 'Get your b— tit out of the way!' (Don't try that today!)

People think that gynaecology is either lascivious, yucky or both. Its fascination is that it encompasses elements of internal medicine, especially endocrinology, surgery, psychology and a sprinkling of general practice. And there is the satisfying challenge of obstetrics.

Later, when I was a senior house officer in the UK, I tried to get a copy of Parry-Jones's definitive textbook on Kielland's forceps. I went to Foyle's Bookshop in London, then said to be the largest bookstore in the world, went to the second-hand medical section and asked a salesman there if they had the book. He was a tall, superior-looking Englishman and, looking down his nose at me, asked if I was a gynaecologist. When I said I was, he said, 'Disgusting business! Disgusting!' I managed to get out of there without bursting out laughing.

The book, originally published by Butterworths, was out of print but the author was living in retirement in Wales and had several copies for sale, the same as the Butterworths edition but without their logo. Thus I have a copy sold and signed by the author himself.

We also lived in for a shorter time for another subject, I think anaesthetics. I liked anaesthetics but did not go on with it as there seemed to be a lot of complex physics and maths to do with lung function when you did it seriously.

Our medical training was very largely theoretical and we were left to pick up the practical aspects, like putting in IV drips, when we got to be resident doctors. This was much to the amusement of the young nurses, whose training was very practical, and in contrast to those of our British colleagues with whom I worked in my intern year who had already mastered such practical skills in their student days.

Anaesthetics, however, was the one field in which we did get some practical hands-on experience. When we graduated as fresh young doctors, probably the only practical medical procedure we could have performed was to administer, maintain and recover a full relaxant anaesthetic, intubation included.

Indeed, I did quite a bit of relatively unsupervised anaesthetics in my second postgraduate year, and during my residency at the Women's Hospital, Crown Street, in my third year out, it was taken for granted that we were competent and we were rostered to anaesthetise for the public gynae operating lists.

At North Shore, we had to rearrange our student groups at the end of fourth year, as there was one group too many. After that, we went through with a student group of friends until final year was on us with the final exams and off to work in the world of hospitals; university days now behind us but a lot more studying yet ahead.

Hospital Residency, Launceston

A relatively new innovation at university was the introduction of a long elective term between fifth and final years. The purpose of this was to give us the opportunity to follow our interests or do something like going to a third world country. Something like work experience towards the end of high school.

Several of us took a relatively easy approach and organised to go to the Old Men's Home associated with Lidcombe Hospital. This was not as useless as it sounds, as that place had more rare pathology among its inmates than you could shake a stick at. Perhaps the funniest anecdote to come from there was the old guy we saw sitting on the doorstep of his dormitory hut and looking out over the tombstones in the adjacent Rookwood cemetery who said to us, 'That's the slowest game of cricket I've ever seen. Those fieldsmen haven't moved for hours.'

One reason I wanted a relatively soft option for the elective term was that, like several others, I had taken advantage of the break to get married.

In final year, we also had to apply for the hospital where we wanted to spend our junior resident (now intern) year or PGY1 (postgraduate year 1). It was also referred to as the pre-registration year, as you were not eligible for full medical registration until you had completed it. Passing the final exam and graduating gave us provisional registration, enabling us to work in that capacity. You had to list the hospitals of your choice according to your priority, and your marks in the final exam determined where you ended up.

However, at that time Tasmania did not have a medical school, so the superintendents of the various Tasmanian hospitals travelled around during final year to recruit potential junior residents for the following year.

This seemed like a good idea to me, as it would be a bit of an adventure and, even more importantly, they provided married accommodation. We all knew that resident doctors worked long hours for a paltry pay cheque, so not having to rent accommodation had its allure. Also, our colleagues had been recruited from medical schools all over Australia and even the UK, so it enlarged our circle.

In those days, it was a matter of pride to work the long hours, something like ninety hours a week, despite the poor pay (there was no overtime). We worked our usual days during the week plus took our turn being on call for nights and also weekends. What a contrast to today! As I kept telling my trainees at Townsville, when I went through, one's postgraduate training was a prelude to one's career. Now, with decent hours and decent pay, the training is much longer and is a part of the career instead of a prelude to it.

Today's system is better. It has gone too far, though. Now, when junior staff work nights, they are rostered on nights for a week and have no daytime duties. Then they are given a week off to recuperate from the night work. However, today's young adults are no less resilient than we were, so they take advantage of this to bolster the bank balance by working somewhere as a locum for the week. When Queensland Health got wind of this, they issued an edict that their current employees were not to be hired as locums at Queensland hospitals. So, instead of working locally during their 'week of rest', they go interstate.

We had a good time at Launceston, although the administration was very corrupt. The dining room staff would eavesdrop on the junior doctors and report back to the medical superintendent. In that system, he was called general superintendent, as he was CEO of the hospital as well as medical director.

We had decided to buy a car and drive down. As we could only afford an old car, we decided it had to be a Holden, as spare parts were very common in case we had a problem in the country somewhere. We got a 1960 FB Holden, which served us well until we sold it to Heather's brother Stan when we went to the UK in 1969.

We drove down to Melbourne, where Heather's brother and his wife were living and working and spent Christmas with them. We then caught the *Princess of Tasmania* car ferry from Melbourne to Devonport. If I remember rightly, we spent overnight on the car ferry and arrived in Devonport in the morning. We then drove to Launceston.

We arrived in Launceston about lunchtime, so we looked for a café in which to eat. We found one, walked in and got a funny look from the woman behind the counter, who asked us what we wanted. I said we were kind of hoping to buy lunch, to which she answered that they were closed for lunch. I said, 'You're a café and closed for lunch?' to which she said, 'The staff have to eat.'

We duly found somewhere else to eat then reported to the hospital administration. It was a day or two before I was due to start work. There was plenty of vacant accommodation in a nurses' home, so I asked if perhaps we could stay there until it was time to start work, when our married quarters would be available. I was told that no hospital accommodation was available to anyone not on the staff and we were not yet on staff.

We found some decent but cheap accommodation down the road at a building that was then a guesthouse, called Morton House. Morton House was the place where the first anaesthetic in Australia had been administered. It was named after Morton, who was a pioneer in anaesthesia, as I knew from having read Thorwald's books almost a decade earlier. It has since been a restaurant, is still there and is heritage-listed.

But worse was to come. Our colleagues were all in the same boat as us. We had come to Launceston as we were just coming out of our student years and had got married. So we wanted the married quarters, which were fine, but students receive no pay, so none of us was exactly flush with money. Part of the deal was that we would be recompensed on arrival to the tune of a single airfare from wherever we were coming from to Launceston. We were all hanging out for that but when we asked for it, we were told that it would be added to our first pay packet, due at the end of the month. Some of us were reduced to literally a few cents (thirty-five cents actually) for several weeks. Fortunately, those worst affected were husband and wife doctor couples, so could both eat in the staff dining room on the top floor, otherwise they would have starved.

Another couple, both doctors – indeed, both students with me at North Shore – and I were the only Sydney graduates among us. This meant that not long after we got to Launceston we had to take a day off and get on a plane to go back to Sydney for our graduation ceremony. Unlike other universities where if your final year is 1966, your degree is dated 1966, Sydney has or had its graduation ceremonies early the following year. Thus although we completed the course in 1966, we are MB, BS 1967.

As usual everywhere, we did rotating residencies of several terms. I spent my first days as a doctor as junior resident to a pair of orthopaedic surgeons, Messrs Hogg and McIntyre. I noticed when in more recent years I visited the new Launceston Hospital that an operating theatre had been named after those two. I wasn't surprised; they were very good. The registrar, an English guy called Leake, nicknamed 'Sprunger,' was not as helpful as he might have been. I think he expected me to have the practical skills that the UK graduates had and resented the effort it took to teach me to put in an IV and so on.

I also worked for another surgeon, a Scot called Huish. He did general surgery but was also trained as a thoracic surgeon, so I got good experience.

For my medical term, I worked for Dr L, from NZ. He was a character! A kind and conscientious man who left no stone unturned and no detail unattended to. Thus he was usually late finishing work. 'My poor wife! My poor wife!' was his usual lament as he grinned and attended to every patient in minute detail past the usual hours. Naturally, he was taken advantage of by his colleagues, who dumped every difficult case on him. One of the patients, to emphasise to me how serious her case was, did so by making sure I knew she was 'a Dr L patient'.

He certainly had his share of nuts and hypochondriacs. I remember one guy, a bald, middle-aged to elderly man who was constantly in hospital. He had several daughters whose duty it was to take it in turns to sit up all night with their father in hospital. There was nothing wrong with him.

Launceston General Hospital was the major hospital to which serious cases were sent from all the northern part of Tasmania. It also had a psychiatric unit where I worked for a short half term. Significant psychiatric problems were sent to the psychiatric hospital in Hobart but the unit at Launceston, the Lindsay Miller Clinic, dealt with those cases that could be helped with a short stay, maximum six weeks. Thus we spent our efforts on people who could be helped and did a great deal of good. I learnt a lot about depression, schizophrenia and such. Many of those we helped were schizophrenics who had neglected their medication and relapsed. We got them back on the straight and narrow and they were able to resume their places as useful members of society. We were able to help folk suffering from depression with appropriate treatment and rehabilitate them until the condition had run its course.

Depression is a serious condition with a death rate from suicide of ten to twenty per cent. Depression is common in the middle-aged to elderly. We helped these folk get better and get their life back. It appears today that if an elderly person is at risk of suicide from depression, there are those agitating for us to help them kill themselves instead of rehabilitating them.

Three personal incidents from the Lindsay Miller Clinic spring to mind.

The senior psychiatrist there was an extroverted chap called Sandy Simpson. Being a friendly character and having a motor boat on which he liked to go fishing, he invited Heather and me to go with him one Saturday. We were minimal drinkers but Sandy liked the odd beer or two. As we were standing on his boat, he said to Heather, in his usual rather bombastic tone, 'Madam, if you would be so kind as to look over that way…I shall have a pee.'

The other psychiatrist was a chap called C, an Irishman who had lived with his wife in Kenya but came to Australia when those African countries became a little less pleasant to live in.

One of my colleagues, Ken Lawson, was into model aircraft, as I was. When Dr C learnt of this he told us that he was into radio-controlled model aircraft also and invited us to go to his house and he would show us his aeromodelling stuff. He told us that we would have no difficulty finding his place as it had a large steel-hulled yacht that he was building in the front yard.

Ken and I turned up at the appointed date and time and knocked on the door. Dr C opened it and looked a bit bemused for a moment, as he had forgotten our date. That was no problem, though, and he very affably said, in his Irish brogue, 'Come on in, boys, we're havin' a Kenya night.'

His wife was away visiting friends in Kenya, for which she was homesick, so he had invited a few of his male friends from Kenya round to his place, where they got nostalgic about Kenya by playing Kenyan jungle sounds on the stereo and telling each other Kenya stories. They were feasting on barbecued chickens they had bought and were drinking whiskey. While they did all that, the two large dogs the Cs had brought with them from Kenya were taking advantage of the effect of the whiskey on their human friends and having a nibble on the chicken pieces that were being waved around as stories were told.

Dr C did take us to his basement workshop and showed us his stuff, which was impressive. I am not sure, though, that he ever finished or flew a radio-controlled plane, or whether he ever finished the boat either.

I had become friendly with a nice guy who was a psychiatric nurse at the clinic and had a pretty good nose for the job. He and his wife were English. I can't remember their names. In those days, indeed still today, Heather and I refer to the evening meal as 'tea', so we invited them round for tea and they duly came and had a meal with us. Shortly after that, they invited us around for tea one evening. Heather and I usually ate a little earlier so by the time we got there, we were starving. Well, we sat and talked and generally had a good time until they brought out some apples to eat. We wolfed a few down and then had a cup of tea.

Thus we learnt that if you are talking about 'tea' with an English person it is as well to be precise in your definition. This knowledge, while hard earned, stood us in good stead when we lived in the UK. We did learn that the English have the same problem and the evening meal goes by different names in different parts of the country.

There are four incidents on the medical side that I won't forget:

In those days, a lot of people were starting to wear seat belts in cars but they had not yet been brought in as law. Thus when I worked in Casualty (Emergency Department, ED, today) I was able to compare the injuries suffered by people brought in from motor vehicle accidents who had worn a seat belt with those who had not worn seat belts. After that, one doesn't want to so much as put the key in the ignition without doing the belt up.

I also noted that a very high percentage of people brought in from motor vehicle accidents, whether drivers, passengers or pedestrians, smelt of alcohol. There were no breathalysers then so I don't know what their actual blood alcohol was but a lot of them – I later learnt eighty per cent – smelt of alcohol. So the campaign to not drink-drive is not without reason.

One time when I was on duty in Casualty, a rather sick little girl was brought in. I had just started to check her out when she sat up, vomited and died. The registrar wanted to know why I had not called him earlier but was satisfied when I told him that I had not even had time for a quick check, let alone time to call him. The poor little kid had an acute meningococcal infection. That's how quickly it can kill. Yet there are those who resist efforts to get people immunised against meningococcus.

And the fourth incident, to finish on a lighter note. I was on call one weekend. I think that meant from around eight a.m. on Saturday morning. There were no urgent duties, maybe a ward round to be done at a convenient time and to be available for other things. On this particular morning, I had slept in a bit. This should not have been a problem, as we were right next door to the hospital and I could always hurriedly pull some clothes on and get there quickly should anything urgent crop up.

It was our duty, when required, to certify people dead when they were brought in in that condition by the ambulance. Even the most obvious situations, such as the guy I had to officially certify dead who had drowned some days before and whose body, half eaten by crabs, had been fished out of the water. The duty doctor had to certify them dead.

At any rate, I was called this Saturday morning to be told that the police had brought in a dead body, so could I please come and certify it so they could get on with their day. I was a bit embarrassed at being late as the police were busy and I didn't want to hold them up.

As I walked up the hospital driveway, I could not see any ambulance. I relaxed a bit as I thought that one of my mates might have seen the ambulance and done the necessary to save time. We did that kind of favour for each other.

I then saw a couple of policemen, who, on seeing me, walked to meet me and said, 'This way, Doctor,' and started to walk towards their police car, a light blue Valiant sedan. I thought, 'Strike, they've got a body in the car!' But the cop veered off towards the boot and I thought, 'Strike, they've got a body in the boot!' He opened the boot and there, in a cardboard carton, was a pile of ashes with a bone sticking out of it! I wasn't going to get caught. I didn't even know for sure that it was a human bone. I therefore certified that the contents of the box in the boot of police car such and such at such and such a time and date, were dead.

Apparently, an old guy had done the usual. Fallen asleep in bed while smoking. I presume also drunk.

There was a resident doctors' lounge on the top floor of the hospital. Heather had fallen pregnant and although her pregnancy was still quite early, her tummy puffed up so that some of my colleagues felt she must be further along when they saw her sitting there as we watched the TV there.

It was about that time that she felt the baby's first kick. It wasn't gentle. Ian knew how to make his presence felt right from the start.

It was while watching TV there on and just after my twenty-fifth birthday, 5 June 1967, that we first saw history being made on TV in the form of the 1967 Arab/Israeli war. Australia had a specific interest in that, not politically but because the Israelis had the French-made Mirage jet fighters that were at the time on order for Australia and it gave our air force a chance to see them in action.

Many people accused Israel of starting that war and being the aggressor. What happened was that the Arab nations surrounding Israel were massing their forces to destroy Israel but Israel pre-empted them by destroying the Egyptian air force on the ground before they could attack. I would call that self-defence myself.

Marriage

Before going any further, I should explain how I came to be married by then. It began in a rather paradoxical fashion.

I have already said that I was distracted in my third year at university and that led to me failing that year and needing to repeat it. It really did take but a moment's lapse of concentration, the medical course being so intense then.

At any rate, the father of the cause of the concentration lapse thought it would be good for me to go to what we then called a camp or houseparty, I can't remember which. Today we would call it a weekend conference. It was put on by an organisation called the Pocket Testament League, which encouraged evangelism by giving away little booklet editions of the Gospel of John to all and sundry whom one came across in the course of a day. Not a bad practice at all.

The camp, I think somewhere around Narrabeen Lakes in the northern beaches area of Sydney, was held in premises consisting of dormitories, kitchen and meeting hall maintained by a dear old busybody lady called Mrs Simms. She really was a character. I remember there was a girl there, somewhat on the plump side and rather plain but quite a pleasant person. This lass needed a lift somewhere and as I had driven there in the Singer, I gave her a ride. Neither she nor I thought anything more of it than that but, as I was a boy and she was a girl and I had driven her in my car, a nod's as good as a wink and I am sure Mrs Simms had us as good as married off and about to start a family.

I thought the conference good enough to go back again the following year, early March 1963. This time I noticed a young, rather shy and attractive blonde girl, Heather Eddington. Heather had been there the previous year also but neither of us remembers the other from then. Heather was obviously highly regarded by the senior members of the Pocket Testament League who knew her well as they had taught her at Sunday school since she was little. At any rate, before the camp was over, I plucked up the courage to ask her for her phone number.

Heather lived way out in the sticks, at Berrilee, on the northern side of Galston Gorge, which was pretty well near the end of the civilised world as we knew it then. She worked in the city, where of course there was a telephone, but there was no phone at her home as yet so the number I got was her work number.

So I took my courage in both hands and gave her a call. I was working at Magnetic Sound then and remember ringing from a public phone at Wynyard Station. I was so tense, but fortunately for me she was alert and just as I was about to hang up, she remembered to ask me where we should meet.

Our first date was dinner at a restaurant called the Roost in George Street, just up from Wynyard but on the other side of the road. It served only chicken dishes and was quite something for those days, as chicken was a bit of a delicacy, unlike today when you can get it in every way, shape and form from the supermarket, Kentucky Fried or anywhere. That was a brave step for me as it may not have been cheap but at least I had been working full-time recently, albeit for only a low wage.

After that, Mum's Hillman Minx put on a fair mileage to Berrilee and back. (The Singer was gone by then.) The first time I took Heather home, she told me to be careful and go slow on a certain stretch of road as it was very bad. I said, 'OK,' but thought I could handle any road conditions. The poor Hillman's suspension got a real workout and I was more careful next time.

After a while, Heather boarded at a house in Edgecliff David Avenue, Hornsby, and commuted to work from there. Mrs Green, her landlady there, was a bit of a character also. She couldn't see very well so to make gardening easier she put plastic flowers in her flower beds. But to look and feel normal, she watered them. One day when I went to pick Heather up and Mrs Green answered the door, she said to me in a conspiratorial whisper, 'You've got competition, you know.' However, the gentleman friend she had seen coming to visit Heather had actually been her brother Stan.

We got on really well. We seemed to be kindred spirits and would sit for hours just talking. It was just nice being with her. We got engaged at the end of 1964 and married a year later, on 29 November 1965.

There was one sad occasion during our courtship. Across the road from where Heather lived at Berrilee there was an elderly widow who lived alone in a very old house. She was called Mrs Ferguson and was a good friend of Heather's mother. One day, Dad was giving me a lift to the station on his way to work. The car radio was on and we heard a newsflash that an elderly woman, Mrs Ferguson, had been found murdered, battered to death in her home at Berrillee.

That was a bit of a shock to the system. Heather would have been on her way to work at that time so when I got to a public phone, I gave her a call at work so she wouldn't first hear of it on the radio.

The police caught the perpetrator through some very clever forensic work, even back in the early 1960s. It was one of the boys Heather had gone to school with. He was unstable and had a list of old women he was going to kill, Heather's mother being next, so it's as well he was caught. I believe he spent twenty years in prison.

Heather lived on a small acreage. Her father had had a chicken farm, as many in that district had, so the eating of a chook wasn't quite so rare in that community as generally. Unfortunately, Heather's parents had split up some time before I met her. That's partly why the folk at the camp knew her so well, as they had taken her under their wing and been surrogate parents to quite an extent.

Heather's mum was a quiet, God-fearing woman who brought Heather up very well in the knowledge of the Lord. She did have her moments, though, that no doubt contributed to the break-up of the marriage. Heather has a sister about thirteen years older than she and a brother about eight years older. Like my own mother, Heather came along later.

Heather's dad was a lovely man. He had been a 'Dreadnought Boy', one of quite a number brought as youngsters to Australia after World War I from the UK to be taught farming skills and given a new chance at life. Perhaps not unlike the Aboriginal Stolen Generation. He was not yet sixteen when he left Edinburgh. His father wasn't around, his mother wasn't that interested and his grandmother brought him up until he was sent off to Australia. He never talked about that. Heather did a lot of family history research many years later.

The lads were sent to a training camp called Scheyville near Pitt Town, north-west of Sydney. Later, we lived on a few acres virtually across the road from there.

When the tensions in the family got too much, Heather's father moved to Hornsby, as he was working for Clark Industries, who made heavy earthmoving machinery.

Unfortunately, although Heather was very bright and actually earned herself a place in a prestigious girls' high school, her dad wasn't a believer in educating women and she went to a domestic home science school, left school after the Intermediate Certificate and joined the workforce. I may have the university education but I can assure you, she has the brains.

Albury, Part 1

Getting there

So there we were. We had gotten married while I was still at university, sharing a little two-room (not two-bedroom) flat in the inner western Sydney suburb of Croydon. We had further defied convention by not applying for one of the local Sydney hospitals for my junior residency but had gone interstate. Where to next?

Most of us juniors at Launceston had enjoyed the year and were happy to stay on for a second year. The unofficial word was that we all could, although I don't remember having that in writing.

I have already made a few remarks about the administration at Launceston. Some of us, such as yours truly, are not smart enough to just put their heads down, keep their mouths shut and quietly carry on. Those who did were given jobs for a second year there. Most of us suddenly found that at short notice we had nowhere to go.

However, one of the benefits of being a junior doctor is that you are not tied down; you can go anywhere they will take you. I thought about this. I had always been a city boy, born and bred. But I wondered if I might not like country life.

I had heard that Albury, on the NSW-Victoria border, and where twenty years before we changed trains in the middle of the night, was a very good place, so I thought, 'Why not? Let's give it a go and find out.' I had nothing to lose, so applied for a senior – that is, second year – residency and was accepted.

So when our time at Launceston was up, we again loaded up the Holden FB (which Heather had also learnt to drive), drove to Devonport again and crossed the Bass Strait on the *Princess of Tasmania*.

As we drove up the Hume Highway towards Albury, a distance of about 325 kilometres, or a little over 200 miles in those days, we had severe heatwave conditions. The poor old Holden kept boiling at frequent, regular intervals. Everywhere we stopped and asked for it to be checked we were told that it was so hot that every car was boiling, just go easy and take your time. At one point, we stopped at a service station where the building was an old corrugated-iron shed. We walked in and said, 'Phew, it's cooler in here.' At which the garage man pointed to the thermometer on the wall and said, 'It's 110.' (That was 110 degrees Fahrenheit, a bit over 43 degrees Celsius.)

I should mention that Heather was about six months pregnant and we also had Chum, our old black Labrador with us. We got him in Launceston when he had been retired from retrieving ducks in the season, as he was getting too old. He made our lives that much happier while we had him. I left him with Dad when we went to England in late 1969. Dad loved him and looked after him until he got cancer and had to be put down while we were overseas.

As the 'cool' of evening approached and the car was about to boil again, we were approaching the town of Benalla, still some 120 kilometres from Albury. Never did a neon motel sign look so good. So we stopped the night and the following morning had the car looked at by a mechanic at a service station next door. He took one look and said, 'No wonder you were boiling. Your radiator's blocked.' It took him no time at all, and not a lot of money, and we had a new radiator core and were on our way. A day late but there nonetheless.

Working there

Our accommodation was half of a very old and dilapidated house, but it did.

The experience at Albury was excellent. There were a couple of us residents and partway through the year a chap just a little older than I, Warwick Williams, came to join us. Warwick had previously been a resident at Albury and was very much liked. He had gone to England to do some obstetrics and came back with a Diploma of Anaesthetics (DA). He later went on to become a well-known psychiatrist.

We were used generally where needed, not in rotating terms attached to specific people. I got good experience in anaesthetics and general surgery and also obstetrics and gynaecology. We were also shown how to do basic pathology tests, which utilised the skills we had learnt in our practical chemistry classes at school and university.

There were no automated machines in those days. Nowadays you put a little blood sample into one end of a machine and within moments it spits out everything about the patient from the other end. In those days, there was a list of instructions on the lab wall for what to do for each test and we did the pathology manually. There were only one or two lab staff, so the doctor on call was also often rostered for out of hours lab tests like typing and cross-matching blood, blood counts, electrolytes, liver function tests and so on. If one had done practical lab chemistry before, it was a simple matter of following the instructions. I was also shown how to do post-mortems and did at least one unsupervised.

As a country town, Albury did not yet have a full complement of specialists and often the path to a rural specialist practice was to be part of a general practice group or partnership and do the specialist work in your field for the group as well as your share of GP. After a while, you got well known enough to go out in full-time specialist practice. The specialists were Bill Stephens, a physician; four general surgeons, of whom two were in full-time specialist pratice; David Nelson, who had recently dropped his share of general practice to do full-time obstetrics and gynaecology; and Ray Bottoms, a mild-mannered orthopaedic surgeon who drove his Jaguar Mark X sedan at a terrifying pace. I nearly forgot Carl Leberne, a urologist with a penchant for avant garde, rather flashy clothes.

The convention at the time was that if a GP referred a patient to a surgeon, the GP would do the anaesthetic when it came time for the surgery. One of the GPs, John Stoney, a member of one of the larger group practices, had his Diploma of Anaesthetics and was quite competent. He was the nearest thing to a specialist anaesthetist and was deferred to as such by other GPs if they had a high-risk anaesthetic patient. It was said that 'Stones', a tall and athletic-looking man, had financially established himself in practice with the prize money he got from the prestigious Stawell Gift foot race some years previously.

Thus we were exposed to the joys of country town GP as well as the various specialties. I got to do quite a few anaesthetics, especially lists for Ray Bottoms. I also got to do enough surgery that the Royal College of Obstetricians and Gynaecologists (RCOG), of which I later became a member, accepted my time at Albury in lieu of a six-month dedicated surgical residency, which was part of their requirements for the membership.

I had shown some interest in obstetrics. I had even delivered a baby at Launceston. There was no obstetric department at the Launceston General, the deliveries then all being done at the separate Victoria Hospital.

I was good friends with David Roberts Thomson and his wife Sally. We went through medicine together, then when we graduated, David went to Hobart while we were at Launceston; they were in Melbourne when we were in Albury; later we were in the UK together and remained good friends until David's untimely death from a brain tumour in 2007 at the age of sixty-nine. We are still good friends with Sally.

David's uncle Hank Roberts Thomson was a senior and highly respected obstetrician/gynaecologist in Launceston and kindly allowed me to do a public delivery at the Victoria when I was off duty from the General Hospital, the first baby I had delivered since I was a student in fifth year and the first one unsupervised.

David Nelson taught me a lot of good stuff at Albury. One day I was leaving the maternity ward there, having just delivered a baby. I felt so good about it that I realised, Hey, *this* is what I want to do.

David looked after Heather in her pregnancy and on 10 April 1968
he helped Heather bring our first son, Ian, into the world at three p.m. weighing in at eight pounds nine ounces or 3.88 kilograms.

Easter was late that year and Heather was still in hospital when Dr Hosking, if I remember his name right, the sole GP at nearby Tallangatta, asked if I could give him a bit of relief by doing a few days locum over Easter. I could do that as I now held full medical registration.

My two enduring memories are firstly of the drive to Tallangatta in the early morning light along the road following the southern shore of Lake Hume. The scenery in that light was just breathtaking. The second is that I was called out to a rural homestead where an old lady had just died. This was a real traditional Australian country homestead, again set in the most glorious countryside. It was one of those lovely old homesteads with verandas all round, high ceilings and furnished with the most beautiful antique furniture. All magnificently kept.

The medical superintendent at Albury was Dr Allan Hogan, who also had his qualifications as a physician. I was intrigued that Allan Barry Hogan had the same initials as Albury Base Hospital, which he headed. Although a doctor, Allan was nevertheless the typical bluff, hard-drinking Aussie country bloke.

Allan was very chuffed when Ian was born. He was the first baby born to a resident doctor in office at Albury Base. Allan told me that boys born in Albury were referred to as 'colts from Albury'. As becomes very obvious very quickly, Albury was a very strong horsy area.

Now my story so far may make it seem that I liked the adventurous life but the truth is that I was, probably still am, a shy, very naive, insecure, socially inept dork. Fifty years later, I still cringe at the memory of the events immediately following Ian's birth.

For almost all my life until then, I had been a non-drinker, a teetotaller. I was just at the point where I had started to look with a little interest at wine and had just about realised there were three varieties: red, white and rosé. I may have had one, or maybe two, small glasses of beer in my life.

Bear in mind that Albury, like most similar towns, was quite 'social.' At any rate, Allan Hogan, together with a few of his cronies from the upper echelons of Albury society, took me to the prestigious Albury Club for 'a drink' to celebrate Ian's birth. I was very appreciative of their hospitality and generosity in buying me drinks, and trying and hoping that I wouldn't drink too much. It never dawned on me that the reason they kept doing it was that they were waiting for me to realise that in due course it was my turn to shout a round.

A less embarrassing but nevertheless telling incident was when we had a middle-aged man come in having just had a heart attack one evening. The sophisticated monitoring machinery we have now wasn't yet invented. Hospital beds had saggy spring bases and, as people were just beginning to learn CPR, most wards were equipped with a bed-sized sheet of plywood, known as a cardiac arrest board, stored somewhere handy to quickly shove under the mattress and provide a firm base for CPR to be done if needed.

This poor guy's heart kept stopping. Fortunately, this was noticed in time every time and a simple thump on the chest got him going again. Obviously, he needed the facilities of a much larger hospital so it was arranged to send him to Melbourne by road ambulance the next morning. I was to accompany him.

A medical escort was an obvious necessity but in reality little more than a gesture. Monitoring equipment wasn't invented yet and it was my intention to keep my finger on his pulse and get the ambulance to pull over if we needed to thump his chest again. I had asked the ambulance driver not to drive too fast, as it is impossible to feel someone's pulse in a moving, jolting vehicle; and to only use their siren and lights if needed to get us through any traffic delays in the towns on the way.

So of course they set off and went all the way to the outskirts of Melbourne at eighty miles an hour (130 kmh), slowing to sixty (100 kmh) through the towns. (The road then wasn't what it is now.)

As we approached the northern outskirts of Melbourne, I saw a

police car waiting for us in a side street some distance ahead. As soon as the cops saw us, they pulled out ahead to clear the way and upped the speed to ninety miles an hour (145 kmh). In the time we had taken to get there, they had blocked off the street, in the morning peak hour traffic, to keep it clear for us. It was a dual carriageway with a median strip, so wherever they had not been able to clear the traffic one way they had done so on the other side and the police car led us onto the wrong side of the road at the preceding intersection break in the median strip.

We got to the Royal Melbourne Hospital fortunately without the guy's heart stopping, as there would have been nothing I could have done to tell if it had, let alone do anything to fix it.

I was a little shaken by the ride and by the time I had alighted from the ambulance and gathered my wits, he had been whisked away. I enquired at the hospital front desk where he was and they directed me to the appropriate floor and I got in the lift and went there.

I asked after him at the nurse's station. They asked me if I was a relative and I said no, I was the doctor from Albury who had accompanied him. They told me what room he was in. It was a single room with the door closed and I asked if anyone, nurse or doctor, was with him. They said no, he was on his own. I asked if there was a cardiac arrest board in the room. They said, 'No. Does he need one?' I said, 'Well, his heart stopped five times last night, that's why he's here.'

I have never seen anyone move so fast to get someone to be with him and a cardiac arrest board under him. We did a good job at Albury, yet the staff at the big-city teaching hospital thought so little of us that they hadn't even listened adequately to the history that had been sent on about this patient.

I noted the same attitude when later I worked at the Hawkesbury Hospital. The standard of care provided there was very high, due in part to the fact that it was a small hospital with few juniors and even fewer trainees, so most care was provided directly by either experienced GPs or qualified specialists. Things went on at the big-city hospitals that would not be tolerated at Hawkesbury. Indeed, the powers that be at the city hospitals would have censured us roundly and possibly tried to close us down had we done some of the things I regularly saw at those hospitals that looked down their noses at us.

My late father's paraplegia due to delay in getting into theatre is a case in point. At Hawkesbury, someone would have had a case cancelled to allow the urgent case to go ahead. I could cite some obstetric cases as well.

Crown Street

As 1968, the year at Albury, came to a close and I had decided to do obstetrics and gynaecology, it was time to look at planning my career path.

The specialist qualification in O&G in those days was membership of the Royal College of Obstetricians and Gynaecologists, the MRCOG. The college was English, of course, with its headquarters in London. It would be ten years before we actually got an Australian College of O&G. There were Australian Colleges of both Surgeons and Physicians but even so just about everybody went to the UK for experience and to obtain membership or, in the case of surgery, fellowship, of the English college.

Crudely put, apart from gaining the letters after our names, the benefit was the vast amount of experience to be gained practising on the natives in the British NHS. The British liked us as we were from a culture with language, medical standards and education similar to their own but, at the end of our training, would return home instead of swelling the long queue of doctors 'waiting to step into dead men's shoes' for a consultant spot in Britain.

When Warwick Williams had gone to England after his initial stint at Albury, before my time, he had secured a position at the Princess Margaret Hospital, Swindon, Wiltshire. That's about halfway across England between London and Bristol. When he learnt that I was intending to go to the UK to further my specialist training, he recommended that I contact them, as the department was very congenial, the experience good and the geographical location very good.

He advised me to write to the head of the Department of O&G there, Mr Gordon Jolly, and gave me the address. Mr Jolly replied very promptly and in a most friendly tone and offered me a job there as senior house officer, to start the following September (1969). That left the first half of 1969 to fill in. Fortunately, I was able to secure a spot as a junior at the Women's Hospital, Crown Street, Sydney.

"Crown Street' was closed in the 1980s by the Wran state Labor government. They had recognised that Sydney's population had shifted significantly to the west and opened the new major hospital at Westmead and closed Crown Street and significantly downgraded Sydney Hospital. They were right, that was correct progress, but it was still a pity, as a lot of history was discarded. Sydney Hospital is the oldest hospital in Australia; Crown Sreet was a women's hospital of world standing. It was the first institution in the world where that dread complication of pregnancy, eclampsia, was first overcome. Earlier in the twentieth century, Crown Street published a series in which there were no cases of eclampsia in a large series of *booked* cases. Thus they showed the preventive value of antenatal care.

Life while at Crown Street was more conventional. We rented a house in Chatswood, overlooking Beauchamp Park, and I commuted in to Crown Street. Work at Crown Street was different in that I now was working full-time in the discipline of O&G. We worked the usual hours and did our share of being on call at nights and weekends as per usual except that the labour ward was run on a different system. We rotated in 'terms' of one week at a time.

There was a resident doctor physically present on the labour ward around the clock. 'Day labour ward' was one term, 'night labour ward' another. Those were seven-day terms of twelve hours each shift, the only time I ever worked in shifts.

Day labour ward was OK as there was always something going on, there were colleagues around for company and we were relieved for a lunch break.

Night labour ward was a drag. We were there twelve hours straight without a break, having had dinner before coming on duty and breakfast after. The registrar was on call, so we only saw him or her if there was a problem. When it was quiet, the midwives would gather chairs in a circle and chat and knit and the resident was ignored.

There was an upside. In the knowledge that it was a soul-destroying term, the powers that be had organised for it to be followed by a week doing the 'annexe' term. The annexes were two or three buildings, I can't remember which, that Crown Street owned and used as maternity homes for single women awaiting their babies in late pregnancy or recuperating from their childbirth, or women from outlying districts and needing longer-term care.

They were established when having a baby out of wedlock was a cause for shame and gave these girls some privacy and dignity. Their real estate value, on the water in the inner eastern suburbs with beautiful views overlooking the harbour, would be astronomical today.

It was assumed you had a car to get to them. The ward rounds only took a couple of hours and then the day was yours, and no night duty that week.

The gynaecology was done on the ground floor of Founders Block at Crown Street. We referred to that week as 'Founders grounders'. We saw very little gynaecology as such; they mainly used us as staff anaesthetists for the public gynae operating lists.

The administration was unique. Obviously there were honoraries (consultants) appointed and each patient was nominally under the care of one of them. However, the honoraries were only ever involved if a caesarean was required. Thus the caesarean section rate for public patients was the lowest I have ever seen at three per cent. We got pretty adept with the forceps, though.

Resident staff, the 'seniors' – that is, registrars – and we 'juniors' were under the authority of a full time medical superintendent who lived in accommodation on the top floor. The recent incumbent had been Vic Pannikote, who was very highly regarded but by the time I got there he had been succeeded by Harry Tischler, also very competent both at his work and as a teacher and quite approachable.

Crown Street had a reputation to maintain and was very jealous of its high standards. There were about five thousand babies born every year, which is a lot. There was also a huge turnover of trainee doctors, medical students and pupil midwives.

The high, uniform standard of care was achieved through strict adherence to rigid guidelines for everything. It was all written down. We juniors had rules about when to call the duty senior and so on. This made for a very rigid environment that I don't think I could have tolerated for too long, but as everything was carefully thought out and had good reason, it not only gave me a very good foundation for later years, but due to the logic behind every rule it was wise to think twice before doing something differently.

We juniors were all minimum third year since graduation. This is because obstetrics has its own challenges and not only is it important to recognise things early but things can go wrong very quickly. It still worries me when I see interns in their first postgraduate year assigned to an obstetric residency.

Two funny stories came out of Crown Sreet.

Breast feeding was encouraged, ostensibly for the usual reasons but really because the formula for a bottle-fed baby had to be made up by the nursery and that was work. If a mother wanted to bottle feed, she had to get permission (*sic*) from the sister in charge of the nursery, the request to be relayed via the resident doctor, who was meant to sort her out so the decision could be justified if she insisted.

One day I was doing my postnatal ward round when a lady, who happened to have breasts like swollen melons, asked me to get permission for her to bottle feed. (She had been there before and knew the ropes.) I asked her why and she replied that this was her third baby, she had tried to breast feed the previous two and it had not worked on either occasion.

I thought that was fair enough so went to the nursery to get the necessary permission. A midwife who was as wide as she was tall and had a moustache met me. I passed on the request and the reason for it, to which she said, 'Humph! All right then. But Sister — is back on tomorrow and you won't find her so lenient!'

In the second incident, I was on call for the hospital one night. That meant handling the few calls there might be from the wards and being available for anyone who came in through the small gynaecological emergency room. The hospital door was never closed but out of hours there was always a security guy.

I got a call to see a girl who had been brought in by her boyfriend. She had lower abdominal pain and bleeding. I asked her as a routine question whether or not she could be pregnant, to which she replied a definite 'No.'

I checked her tummy and found the bulge of a sixteen-week pregnant uterus so I asked her again and again she denied it.

I was young and unsure of how to handle this situation, not the medical side but the fact that a patient was denying the obvious. I called Jules Black, the registrar on call, and told him the score before he went into the room.

Jules went in and again asked her whether she might be pregnant and she again denied it. He then told her that Dr Kraus was of the opinion that she was sixteen weeks pregnant, in such a way that I felt quite complimented by the way he said it, and told her he thought so too.

I can't remember further medical details, although obviously she was miscarrying. However, the funny part of the story is that she and her boyfriend had come tearing into the hospital and headed straight for the lifts. The security guy intercepted them and asked where they were going in such a hurry, to which they replied, 'Labour ward!' He redirected them to the emergency room. And yet they vehemently denied, to two doctors in a women's hospital, one of them obviously senior, that she could possibly be pregnant.

There was a short time between when the six months at Crown Street had finished and when we were due to leave for England on 3 August, the day before Heather's birthday, which she celebrated at our first stop in Hong Kong.

We were staying in the cottage in Chatswood. It was actually owned by St Barnabas Church, where we had been married and where I had gone until then and my parents still attended. They had bought the cottage to be able to help those who might need accommodation but it really was a bit of a run-down disgrace.

My parents had decided to go on an overseas trip but instead of getting us to move back into the home, they got an elderly Hungarian lady Mum knew to house-sit and look after the dog. The problem was that the dog got pregnant and had pups while they were away. It was quite funny as Heather was on the phone to me when I was on night labour ward at Crown Street. It was a quiet night for us but she had six deliveries at home.

The old lady had no idea of looking after a bitch and puppies and Heather had our household to run, including a rather active toddler, so she wasn't too happy to run back and forth between the two places. So enough was enough. Despite the protests of the old lady, who had strict instructions that she, not we, should look after the old family home, we moved in, and she, throwing her hands up and rolling her eyes, moved out.

That was fine but Mum and Dad were due back a couple of weeks before we were due to go overseas. That problem was solved when a colleague whom I had met a few times and who must have heard we were at a loose end, rang me. Apparently he had agreed to do a locum for a few weeks for old Dr Bill Skinner, the then incumbent of the historic convict era 'Doctor's House' in Windsor, north-west of Sydney. Something had happened and he had to leave a week or ten days before Dr Bill got back, so he was stuck.

(The Doctor's House was originally built 1819 as an inn. The present building, completed in 1844 and one of the best examples of colonial architecture, was lived in by a doctor from 1876 until Bill Skinner's retirement in 1992.)

So we found ourselves living in a historic and very old house, doing a GP locum for a doctor whom we hadn't met yet. All went well, though, apart from us thinking the house must be haunted when one night we heard loud creaking footsteps on the stairs to the attic. Quite scary, but it turned out to be the Siamese cats wandering about up there.

We were there and I was seeing patients on 20 July 1969 when Neil Armstrong first set foot on the moon. We made sure Bill's TV set could be clearly seen in the waiting area and I paused between patients so we could all watch this monumentally historic moment. It rather surprised me that a few of the patients were more put out by having to wait a few extra minutes than they were interested in watching such history being made.

England

So on 3 August 1969, Heather and I with sixteen-month-old Ian got on a Qantas B707 to go to England, where I could study and gain my qualifications in the specialty to which I aspired and to actually be in the country of my boyhood heroes.

We found that 1969 was the tenth anniversary of the use by Qantas of the Boeing jet for this route, the much vaunted 'Kangaroo Route'. That made the trip so much shorter and more doable. Before then, the flight was a series of hops, taking several days at relatively slow speed in the magnificent Lockheed Super Constellations. Even in the mid to late 1960s, many people chose to spend three or four weeks in relative luxury on board ship instead of flying, but with the advent of the jet airliner those days were numbered and the earth was shrunk.

The 707 did not have the range of our modern aircraft and made several stops for refuelling. On the normal ticket, which we had, you could make two stopovers. We stopped four nights in Hong Kong and saw the sights, and I think about a week in Athens, during which time we did a four-day trip down to Corinth, Olympia and other such places which were the stuff of legend to us. It was quite something to be where the Apostle Paul had been and to where he had written two letters.

Then it was a short flight from Athens to London and there we were. We stayed at a hotel in London for a few days. London! So redolent in history, and so meaningful to me who as a migrant child had identified so fiercely with the culture of my adopted land, which as already mentioned, was ninety-five per cent British stock and a proud member of the British Empire, by then the Commonwealth.

As someone said to me later when we discussed this, I was just a tad naïve and soon came down to earth with a thud. At that time, some thirty years after the Blitz, there were still areas of unrepaired bomb damage in spots. In contrast, when we later drove around Holland and parts of Germany, it was all new and rebuilt. I suspect there is more than a grain of truth in the pop song 'Right said Fred'. You never got a job done right the first time by a tradesman.

Nevertheless, it was wonderful to be right there under Big Ben, to walk across the Thames on Westminster Bridge, to see Piccadilly Circus and Trafalgar Square. And in the Science Museum at South Kensington I saw not only Stephenson's Rocket, the early locomotive about which I had read in my encyclopaedias as a boy, but also the actual S6B aircraft that had won the Schneider Trophy outright for England and was an important ancestor of the famous Spitfire. I had to pinch myself to be sure I wasn't dreaming.

Then it was off to Swindon. Swindon is about seventy miles (110 kilometres) from London, about an hour on comfortable British Rail trains from Paddington Station. Swindon has a great railway heritage and there is a locomotive museum there.

Swindon, although no beauty spot itself, is handy to so many of Britain's most beautiful attractions. It lies at the northern end of the Salisbury Plain, Salisbury with its cathedral being at the southern edge. It is within reach of Bath, Wantage, the Ridgeway with the Wayland Smithy, Oxford, the Cotswolds, Castle Combe, voted the prettiest village in England, several white horses, Uffington Castle. the Great Coxwell Tithe Barn. Stonehenge. Avebury. The list goes on.

The Princess Margaret Hospital was only five years old, and nice and modern. The maternity unit was a separate building attached to it and had its own operating theatre so Caesareans didn't have to wait or interrupt other booked operating lists. We also did some minor surgery there, like post-partum sterilisations.

The gynaecology was done in the Victoria Hospital, a little way down the road. It was an older hospital in an older area but quite satisfactory. The orthopaedic department was downstairs and gynae-cology upstairs. As one wag put it, 'PID' meant 'prolapsed inter- vertebral disc' downstairs and 'pelvic inflammatory disease' upstairs.

My first six months at Swindon were spent as SHO in gynaecology at the Victoria Hospital. However, the duties included covering the obstetrics when on call out of hours and weekends.

Our accommodation there was in a semidetached cottage in Kent Road, just a short distance from the Victoria. This was two-storeyed. We had the ground floor and a surgical registrar, Arnold Graham Smith, was upstairs. We shared the front entrance. Arnold was single with a semi live-in girlfriend called 'Fred'. Arnold wasn't a bad guy and we got on well. The only clue to the fact that he might put on airs and graces was that the Graham wasn't part of a double-barrelled surname, as he tried to give the impression, but was actually his middle name. I noticed via the internet recently that he ended up as an orthopaedic surgeon in the US.

The accommodation would be best described as 'quaint'. It was just like the houses in the *Coronation Street* soap opera of the day. We realised why the English didn't bathe too often. Try as we might, and we tried hard for the sake of little Ian, we could not get the temperature in the bathroom above forty degrees F (4.5 C) in the winter.

The house was centrally heated, after a fashion. It had a coal-burning furnace with a thermostat, which pumped hot water through radiators in the rooms. There was a little guy, employed by the hospital, who came by on his bicycle at regular intervals. He would put a little coal in the furnace and set the thermostat. After he had been, I would go out, put a little more coal in the furnace and set the thermostat back up a bit higher. He would put it back down on his next round and so on. We realised that he was probably being more generous with us than he would be in his own home.

When later I worked at the Maternity of Princess Margaret as my day job, we were moved to accommodation beside the maternity unit. There was a lovely row of three bungalows, not individually detached. These had been built when the hospital was, so were quite new. They had underfloor central heating, large glass walls looking out onto a yard, and beautiful Cotswold stone in the walls separating the yards.

I had expected the English to be a bit aloof, like the story of the two Englishmen marooned on a desert island who never spoke to each other because they hadn't been introduced. We found that everyone was actually most friendly.

The nearest to an exception to that was when, soon after arrival, I found the local hobby shop. I asked if there was a local model flying club and the proprietor told me I was in luck as the club president just happened to be in the shop then. I shook hands and said I was Peter Kraus, to which he responded, 'I'm Mr Smith.' However, he told me where and when the club flew, at the old Wroughton RAF base, and I was made very welcome. I soon found that one works far too hard as a junior doctor in the NHS to get the time and energy to fly models. I did, however, get to aircraft museums and air shows, both full size and model, which were wonderful.

One of the attractions of Swindon's central location was that we had staff, both nurses and junior doctors, from all over the place. It did not take me long to be able to tell where someone came from by their accent. Sadly, I have now lost that skill. I also learnt to differentiate the different Australian capital city accents.

There was a junior medical staff common room in the basement of the main hospital where English (read 'warm') beer was on tap in either pints or half-pints and there was always a convivial spirit.

About that time, Heather got caught by the 'two countries separated by a common language' thing. Soon after arrival in a new country. one is always susceptible to any bugs going around. She was laid low by a bad cold and did not surface for a few days. In Australia. the slang term for such an ailment is a 'wog'.

When she surfaced and caught up with the other doctors' wives, the girls took one look at her and said, 'You're looking a little peaky today dear. Are you feeling poorly?' To which she replied, rather nonchalantly, 'I'm OK. I've just been in bed for three days with a wog.'

Oxford

Swindon is about thirty miles, at that time about an hour's drive, from Oxford and at that time in Oxford's health service district. (It later got transferred to Southampton.)

Oxford is one of the world's top places for obstetrics, so being at Swindon we were trained in the Oxford district. Furthermore, during term time we went to the Monday evening postgraduate lectures at the famous Radcliffe Infirmary organised by the then incumbent professor of O&G there, Professor John Stallworthy. He had followed the great Professor Chassar-Moir, whom I had the privilege of meeting once and under whom one of our consultants, Michael Yates, had trained.

Oxford is also one of the great tourist attractions of England, redolent with history, beautiful old buildings, historic sites and even Blackwells bookshop and publisher. Not to mention the university buildings spread through the town.

Work at Swindon

I was employed as senior house officer (SHO) at Swindon. That determined the pay rate – a pittance, but at least married quarters were included. Otherwise, SHO meant different things at different places. At Swindon I was virtually a junior registrar but when I was a registrar later at Harlow I had two SHOs under me, one of whom was doing their first six months obstetrics. At Swindon we had a couple of house officers under us in that position.

We were not eligible for overtime until we worked 208 hours a fortnight, and even then only if we had been asked to do the overtime. This time included hours on call. Working a one in two roster made up those hours and I did that for our entire time in England. In some places where they had the staff, it was a one in three roster. Bear in mind that I was studying for the college membership as well. Little Ian asked Heather, 'Mummy, why does Daddy fall asleep at dinner?'

We worked well together, with one exception whom I shall discuss shortly. Many of the house officers under us were doing six months obstetrics to broaden their understanding when they did anaesthetics or surgery. Several of them became lifelong friends with whom we are still in touch.

The other SHO was an Indian from South Africa called Abdul Bulbulia. While he had a most unlikely, but true, name he was a good doctor, good family man and good friend and colleague. He was married to an Irish girl, Catherine, who later became a member of parliament in Ireland.

There were a lot of Indians among the doctors. Those Indians who came from India were a mixed bag, some very good, some terrible and most in between. Like everyone else, you had to get to know them. There were, however, a lot of Indians displaced from various African countries. Without exception, these were all absolutely top notch and the racist policies that forced them out of Africa were to the detriment of those countries.

Abdul was one of them. I shall never forget the time he had just returned from taking his family on holiday in Spain, which was where the English went for a bit of sunshine. I was speaking to him on the phone and asked how his holiday had been. He said, in his delightful accent, 'Oh it was wonderful. The children are brrown as berrries.' (I laughed and said, 'Abdul, they are always brown,' to which he replied, 'Well, they are browner.'

The Consultants

Gordon Jolly was the senior man at Swindon. I believe he was forty-seven at the time. A really nice guy who pretended to hide behind a pretentious manner at times and never succeeded. My observations indicated that he was much underrated. No one had any negative feelings towards him or his work and he was humble, but as time progressed I realised just how good he really was.

He loved his falcons and indeed all wildlife. He was very understanding of his patients. I remember one time when he tried to explain to us why a young lady was in the family way, he said, 'You know; when the blood runs hot in the back seat of the Mini...'

He was married to Enid, a lady of haughty appearance and strident tones with a heart of gold and a foot of lead when driving. Very happily and faithfully married, Gordon would try and make us think ill of him by making slightly double entendre references to their au pair.

Gordon's mother had been Australian and he paid several visits to Australia, where we hosted him and Enid, and later we stayed with them at their beautiful stone cottage in the lovely Saxon town (*not* village) of Cricklade. We last saw him and Enid at their home in 2006 and Gordon passed away not long after.

Michael Yates was forty-five and had been a Fellow at Oxford under the redoubtable Professor Chassar-Moir. He had the lion's share of the private practice at Swindon. He was a tall well-built Yorkshire man who was in the village cricket club and drove a Mini Cooper. I cannot understand to this day how a man his size could fit into it.

The third consultant was a slim, dark-haired, mercurial Welshman, Vyvyan Jones. Vyv was 'near as dammit thirty-eight' when I started work at Swindon. He had not been there long himself and for a while had a bit of a chip on his shoulder. Like everyone else in the NHS, he had got his qualifications then spent years cooling his heels as a senior registrar, doing all the work while the consultant read the *Times*. His appointment at Swindon came about as Swindon really needed a second registrar but the

NHS, in view of the numbers of people like Vyv waiting in the wings, said to Gordon, 'You can't have another registrar but we'll let you have another consultant.'

So poor Vyv, instead of being able to tell a registrar or senior registrar to 'carry on' while he read the *Times*, had to keep doing what he had done for so long, come out at night and bail out the likes of me! However, as we worked together, over very little time we developed a very good and friendly working relationship and later personal friendship.

Vyv was a heavy smoker and a superb and extremely quick surgeon and I learnt a lot from him. The question was, 'Why does Mr Jones operate so fast?' The answer: 'So he can have his next cigarette.' He did give up smoking late in life but sadly this magnificent surgeon went blind from macular degeneration in his retirement.

Once, when he was in a bit of a mood, I assisted him at an abdominal hysterectomy, an operation that usually takes a good surgeon, if no difficulties are encountered, about an hour. Vyv did this one in just over thirty minutes and I was extremely proud that I had been able to keep up with him.

He told me that his fastest time for a caesarean had been seventeen and a half minutes. I once managed eighteen minutes as a registrar and considered myself morally on a par, as on that occasion the scrub nurse was a slow one. It was not until about thirty-five years later that I broke that record with one in seventeen minutes when we were in a hurry to get to an important lecture and the anaesthetist had fiddled around and wasted time. I let Vyv know and he didn't mind. By the way, neither of us ever cut any corners in our surgical techniques.

The Registrar

The registrar when we arrived at Swindon was an Indian chap called Mozumder. He had his MRCOG and went back to India soon after we arrived, so I didn't really get to know him. He was succeeded by ABC – obviously not his real initials but it is best not to give even a hint that might establish his true identity, even though I believe he has now passed away. I'll take the risk that describing him and things about him might identify him. There can't have been two like him. In the English vernacular of the day, I have dined out many times on stories involving him.

To say ABC was weird would be the grossest understatement. At forty-five, he was older than most trainees, in fact, he was the same age as Michael Yates and older than Vyv Jones. He had done a lot of GP obstetrics in rural England, worked in the army and done a lot of third world obstetrics in pre-Gaddafi Libya, where years back he had actually run across Gordon Jolly once. I think he secretly, or perhaps not so secretly, thought himself superior to the consultants due to his 'age and experience'. He said to me once, 'Don't forget, Peter, that for every year of experience you've got, I've got seven.'

Another memorable quote, acting the stiff upper lip Englishman, 'I allow myself emotions…sometimes.' He was serious. Seriously? ABC's given names were the same for all firstborn males of his family and his own son had the same name. Each was distinguished by a variation on the name. For example, had his name been, say, Jonathan, which it wasn't, he could have been known as Jonathon, Jon or Jonnie. And these firstborns were known by a variation of either the first or second given name so there was no confusion as to who was who.

His issues arose from a combination of his arrogance, manual dexterity in obstetric manoeuvres of yesteryear and his contempt for the loss of those skills by the current generation.

What was relevant to do in yesteryear's obstetrics – for example, for the medical reader, internal podalic version to breech, pulling down a leg and hanging a weight consisting of one blade of a Kielland's forceps on it (just the right weight) – may have been the best that was available many decades previously in our society for the management of low-grade placenta praevia. It may well have been useful in Libya, where loss of an infant in childbirth was accepted and common and Caesareans were to be avoided if at all possible, due to the lack of antenatal and other obstetric care for future pregnancies. It was *not* appropriate in 1970 England, yet I saw him do it. To demonstrate his superior skills.

To my pleasant but short-lived surprise and admiration, as ABC studied for the MRCOG exam, he seemed to change his practice to be in line with modern thinking. Sadly, though, the moment he passed his exam and had the letters after his name, he reverted immediately to his previous ways. All his training had been for naught. Except to get the letters after his name.

I learnt that he later joined the RAF as an O&G. Unlike the Australian military, which provides medical care to its members only, the British military also provided care for the wives and families.

Years later, I met a colleague who had at one time served in the Royal Navy. On the off-chance that he might have known ABC, as there can't have been too many O&Gs in the British military at any given time, I asked him if he had ever met ABC? He said, 'Oh him? Yes, he was causing disasters wherever he went.'

Abdul and I, as de facto junior registrars, worked a one in two roster. ABC was also on duty, between the consultant and us, on alternate nights but as we handled most of it, we actually greatly reduced his workload.

What would have been a much more equitable arrangement, and made life so much easier for Abdul and me, would have been if we worked a one in three roster. ABC, who was studying for the MRCOG, said to us, 'Abdul and Peter, I really appreciate what you're doing and giving me the better opportunity to study. Once I have that exam, we'll go on a one in three roster and give you a bit of a break.'

Time passed, he got his membership, and the roster didn't change. We pointed this out to him, to which he said, and I quote verbatim, 'It is beneath my dignity to be on the same roster as people so inferior to myself in age and experience.'

Having said that, he really was very adept with his manual dexterity skills and taught me a lot that subsequently stood me in good stead.

Unfortunately, a combination of all those factors caused me to make the most dreadful mistake of my life.

One evening we had a woman in labour with her first baby, which was presenting as a breech, bottom first instead of headfirst. The legs were extended which tends to make things harder as they splint the body and stop it from flexing sideways.

Delivering a baby by the breech required manual dexterity skills that frankly I was quite good at and enjoyed doing. Nevertheless, for it to be safe, one had to be very careful. The alternative was to do a Caesarean, which was not done as readily then as now. Caesarean section is now the norm for breech babies and, as the statistics show, rightly so.

Apart from careful assessment of the patient beforehand, one had to watch the progress of the labour. If it went quickly and smoothly, one knew all would be well. If, however, progress was slow, then that was nature's way of telling us that a Caesarean was advisable.

On this occasion, progress was slow and in my opinion it would have been wise to bail out and do a Caesarean. Had ABC not been on call, I would have called the consultant and let him know. However, on this occasion, ABC was on call. I knew that if I rang him, he would just denigrate me, tell me I didn't have his skills, and come and do a difficult breech delivery himself. No way would he have done a Caesarean. I knew that then and to this day I am sure I was correct in that assessment. So I didn't ring him but waited out the slow progress and successfully and competently carried out the necessary manoeuvres to deliver the baby. The only problem was that the baby did not survive. It was stillborn. Not due to any lack of skill on my part in the delivery, but due to me not listening to what nature was saying with the slow progress.

For the technically minded, the problem is that if it is a tight squeeze, the aftercoming head has to undergo too much moulding too quickly, causing a tear of the membranes around the brain, with consequent haemorrhage.

I was terribly upset. I looked into the side room where the midwives had put the baby. One of the midwives had put a flower into the little hands. I broke down and cried, and nearly do so again now thinking about it over forty years later.

The buck of course stops with the consultant, who on this occasion was Michael Yates. The next day, he called me into his office to discuss the case and ask why I had not called the registrar. I cannot forget his decency, understanding and kindness. Although he sat at his desk, I remember that I stood beside him, not on the other side of the desk – body language to put me at ease. I explained to him that I knew that ABC would not have allowed a Caesarean, so I felt it might as well be me who got the experience of the difficult breech delivery, which was going to be done anyway. He accepted the explanation. I guess that indicated that he understood what ABC was like.

Years later, when I was a consultant at Townsville, I found that we consultants as a group have a great reluctance to give negative reports on trainees, especially at registrar level. Not good. We are too soft. Maybe it's changing over the time since I have retired.

In maybe late July 1970 or thereabouts, Heather and I had our suspicions and I took a urine specimen to the Victoria Hospital, where I did the simple little test. It was the latest thing, picking up pregnancies as early as five weeks. Today's tests are much more sensitive. It was positive – my first introduction to our second son, Andrew. Michael Yates walked by and asked what I was doing, so I told him. He was the first to congratulate me.

Ultrasound was still in the process of being invented, was very crude and only available at research places. A lot of the early work on it was starting to be done by Professor Donald at Glasgow at about that time. So we had no certainty about when Heather was due, but looking at the date he was born, it would be my guess he would have been conceived about the time of my birthday.

Looking To Move On

We worked very hard at Swindon. I really got superb teaching from the three consultants there and I believe that was the most significant part of my formative training years.

Many years later, one of my registrars at Townsville told me that I was an excellent teacher. That was a nice compliment, which I appreciated. The reason I appreciated it most, though, was that the only way you can really thank those who taught you is to pass that teaching on to the next generation. I really do feel a great deal of gratitude as well as affection for those three consultants who put up with me, took me under their wing, taught me so much and so well and subsequently became friends whom we saw when in the UK, as well as seeing Gordon and Enid in Australia. On one occasion, Vyv Jones and his wife Joan also came out to Australia and visited us. My registrar's comment indicated that I was successful in discharging my debt to my teachers and that was very satisfying.

As my experience grew, the time for me to move on was approaching. There was no fixed training program for the specialty in those days. You simply had to fulfil the College's requirements of working for a certain minimum time in accredited positions, having a book of case reports and commentaries accepted by the College and then passing the exam.

The usual next step was to apply for a registrar post. I wasn't going to get one without references from my consultants, who had to feel I was ready. I felt very chuffed when Vyv Jones said, 'I'll be happy to give you a reference, Peter.' The other two obviously felt the same.

There was, however, another option. Michael Yates was Oxford trained and being Oxford trained would have been a huge feather in my cap for the rest of my career. Michael had tried several times to get nominees from among Swindon's trainees accepted for a post 'at the bottom of the greasy pole' in Oxford. He tried to get me a position there; I was interviewed and offered a post.

That gave me cause to think very deeply as it wasn't as straightforward as all that. A registrar post, apart from giving the next step up in salary, would give me a lot more autonomy and surgery.

I would have started at Oxford for the first six months as a house officer, a step down from an already pitiably low salary scale, and accommodation, married or otherwise, was not included. Furthermore, the numbers of registrars and other trainees were such that people at registrar level were said to be fighting each other to do minor surgery which the house officers under me at Swindon were doing unsupervised. Was it really worth it?

I decided that it wasn't, declined the offer, much to the chagrin of the guy at Oxford but not as much to the disappointment of Michael Yates as I feared, and sought a registrar position elsewhere.

I have made a lot of mistakes in my career choices and for a long time felt that decision was one of them. Lately, I am not so sure.

Heather and I are friends with a colleague who did go through the Oxford system. This is a Chinese colleague who, together with his wife, is very entrepreneurial. They tell the story that all they could afford to rent was a tiny one-bedroom apartment. They sublet the main bedroom and slept in the nook under the stairs. Being Chinese, she approached a Chinese restaurant and did some work there in exchange for some food. We had an active two-year-old, another child on the way, and I'm not sure my nerves could have taken the stress either.

I understand from what other colleagues have said since that receiving a good proportion of one's training in the Oxford region, such as Swindon, and attending postgraduate meetings at Oxford probably allows one to call one's self Oxford trained.

I was shortlisted for several registrar positions for which I applied. This meant they paid for my fares there and back for an interview, but the cost of the fare would be forfeited if I was offered the job and declined it.

The first post for which I was interviewed was at Bellshill in Scotland, near Glasgow. Heather and I spent the money for the fare, not on a train ticket but to drive up, stopping one night at a hotel on the way.

Bellshill was cold, industrial, gloomy. And *cold*. At the interview I asked if, being close to Glasgow and Professor Donald's famous unit, Bellshill had any link with them for postgraduate education, as Swindon did with Oxford? 'No,' was the reply, 'They are Glasgow and we are Bellshill.'

There was only one other candidate for the job and I was terribly afraid I would be offered it, in which case I would either have to take it or pay back the fare money. I can't remember ever being as relieved as when they offered the job to the other candidate. Maybe they realised I was likely to decline it.

Heather had waited in the car and as she saw me come out with a big grin on my face, she didn't know whether that meant I had been successful in my application or the opposite. I think she was as relieved as I that I had not been offered it.

To save a hotel bill on the way back to Swindon and to get there quicker, we decided to drive straight through. There were services every sixty miles on the motorway, so we stopped every hour, stretched our legs and changed drivers. Ian slept in his carrycot on the back seat.

I was shortlisted for an interview at Newcastle, a highly regarded unit with a tradition of having an Australian registrar.

I had some difficulty getting there due to weather, and one of the two consultants who interviewed me gave me a bit of a hard time over that. I was not offered that job either. I was told soon after that it was a good thing it had not been offered to me. Apparently, the two consultants there each had their preferred candidate. I was preferred by one of the consultants but not the other. Had I been given that job, I would have constantly been given a hard time by the other.

I went for another interview at Redhill in Surrey, just south of London, for a position as registrar to a lady gynaecologist, Miss Frith. The job would have been fine but I was heavily outgunned by the other candidate, who had more experience than I and already held the membership.

Harlow

I daresay that I could have gone for a bigger place with a better roster but the truth was that I was really relatively inexperienced for a British registrar post and did not have my membership yet. I was shortlisted for an interview at Harlow New Town, now just Harlow.

Harlow is a small township just north of London with some historic sites. Beside it is Harlow New Town. Harlow and Basildon (where Basildon Bond paper is made) are postwar purpose-built new cities. Harlow was the next place north after Epping, Epping being the northernmost station on the London tube system (Central Line). You caught a country train on the Cambridge line to get to Harlow.

The O&G department was congenial. There was one registrar and two SHOs, one of whom was doing their first six months of obstetrics and therefore as yet inexperienced. Epping Hospital, a little to the south, was run by the same administration and had the same consultants and same staffing arrangements. It was again a one in two roster, the registrars from the two hospitals covering both places out of hours and weekends. The two SHOs were rostered such that the more experienced was on call at the hospital where the registrar wasn't, but had to travel to if needed. This was by no means a unique arrangement in the UK at the time.

Quite nice married quarters were provided in a building in the hospital grounds, right next door to the maternity and main hospital. Four two-bedroom apartments in the building, two upstairs, two down. No garage for the car but it could be parked on the street, which was inside the hospital compound.

I had come early for the interview so I could have a look around, was offered the post and accepted it.

The consultant who did most of the work was Mr Gerald Banwell. He looked after both Epping and Harlow and had rooms in Harley Street. There was another part-time consultant, Stanley Hans, who did some gynaecology but no obstetrics there. He was a very good surgeon but surprisingly conservative in his surgery, always keeping things as simple as he could and doing the minimum necessary. There was a lady gynaecologist, Rita Harrison. She was an Australian married to a British sea captain and helped out with the workload on occasions part time. A nice person and competent but not there very much.

The maternity had a GP unit where the GP obstetricians were autonomous but had the registrar to call on if need be. They did a good job. I don't remember ever being called unnecessarily or not being called when I should have been. They were a pleasant bunch as well.

Thus Gerald Banwell was spread pretty thin, which meant that I pretty well ran the unit. He told me to never hesitate to call if ever I felt I needed to, and he meant it. He was never upset at being called and I never felt alone. The only thing he required me to definitely ring him for was if I wanted to do a Caesarean. He never disputed my decision, though.

It was as well my old chiefs at Swindon had taught me to operate. The usual practice at Swindon was that once I was at the point I could do, say, a hysterectomy, as each operating list had two major cases booked and several minors, the consultant would do one major with me, Abdul or ABC assisting, depending on who was rostered for the list, and the second was done by the junior with the consultant assisting. Thus I had never done a major operation without the consultant scrubbed and assisting.

In my first week at Harlow, on the first operating session I attended, I was shown into the theatre suite where there were two operating theatres. 'That one's Mr Banwell's, that one is yours. Here's your list.' So there I was, right from the get go, doing an operating list with the SHO assisting and the consultant, not unavailable, but scrubbed up and doing his own surgery next door. Ah, at last! That's what being a registrar in England was all about.

I recall one occasion when I had to ask Gerald for help in the middle of a procedure while I was fairly new but by and large I didn't need to. Gerald was a safe operator but neither quick nor brilliant. Much later, I got to know the professor at Westmead quite well. He was an Englishman who was a brilliant surgeon and quite outspoken. It turned out that he had known Gerald in the UK and said of him, 'Can't operate for nuts, though.' Not quite a fair assessment but in those days we did tubal ligations (female sterilisations) by open operation.

I remember one time both of us started a tubal ligation at the same time. I had completed the operation, taken off the gown and gloves and wandered into Gerald's theatre next door to find he had just about done opening the abdomen. He was meticulous and fussy, which means not quick but safe. On reflection, I wonder if it was not tactless of me to wander into his theatre, considering I had finished and he was barely getting started. The arrogance of youth, I suppose.

Gerald was a Christian who was not afraid to say so and set and maintained a high moral standard. He delivered our second son Andrew one night just after he had finished choir practice. There was some question as to whether he would get there in time. Fortunately, he did and saved a friendly dispute between the midwife and me as to who would do the delivery if Gerald didn't make it.

Gerald visited us once when he was in Australia and we lived on a few acres in the Hawkesbury district so he was able to meet Andrew, by then in his late teens, whom he had delivered. Sadly he died of leukaemia far too early at the age of sixty-three.

The midwives were a great bunch. We got along very well, with good teamwork and mutual trust and respect. That's how it should be but so rarely is. There will always be staff with whom it is a pleasure to work and thus provide optimal patient care as well as a good work environment for all. Of recent times, this has sadly become less common, to an alarming and concerning degree.

I again worked far too hard. It was not uncommon for me to see a shift of midwives come on duty, finish their shift, be replaced by the next shift, then come back for their next shift and finish it while I was still there and hadn't left the place or slept. Add to that the pressure to study and I'm sure I became a bit cranky and difficult at times. They must have understood, as they always remained very friendly.

Having a good relationship with the midwives can have its funny side. At one time, I suddenly found them very aloof, stand-offish and playing 'no speaks' with me. It took me a while to find out why and then we all had a good laugh.

At the time, one of our SHOs was a blonde girl who wore her hair up on her head. Heather is blonde and had let her hair grow long and wore it down past her shoulders. One evening as I was walking home, which was next door, I looked over to a grove of trees and saw some squirrels. We don't get them in Australia and I don't remember seeing many in Swindon, so I called out to Heather to come and look at them with me, which she did. The only problem was that on that day she had put her hair up. So the midwives, looking out the window of the maternity unit, saw me in the distance with my arm around the waist of a blonde girl with her hair up on her head. A case of mistaken identity that gave us all a laugh in the end.

Europe

Although we worked hard with a lot of time rostered on duty, at least we had some holidays from time to time.

There were a lot of Dutch migrants in the area where Heather was a girl and she went to school with their kids. Thus when we were living in the southern part of England, Heather wanted to go and see Holland, where her school friends had come from. The idea of seeing Holland would never have occurred to me but I am very glad it did to Heather, as it turned out to be a beautiful and interesting place.

Back in Albury, Warwick Williams had regaled us with stories of the fun times he and his wife had had in the UK and Europe driving everywhere in their Minivan. I had checked them out and thought they might be a bit small for us so had settled on an MG 1100. The same thing as a Morris 1100 but with two carburettors and an MG badge and grille. It was fun. We had bought the MG soon after arrival in Swindon so we could see the countryside. We now bought it a roof rack and ourselves a tent and set off for the car ferry to the Hook of Holland and a new adventure.

We saw a lot in our short time. Beautiful places like Amsterdam, where we celebrated Ian's second birthday, Rotterdam, the Hague, Delft. We loved the Rijksmuseum, where we saw so many magnificent works by Rembrandt. We drove to Gouda, where the cheese comes from. A colleague, John Vett, a bit older than us but nevertheless a junior resident with us at Launceston, was of Dutch origin and we visited him and his wife there. But not until we got over some difficulty in getting directions due to my inability to pronounce 'Gouda' the way the Dutch do.

One disappointment about the cheese was that Edam cheese,

famous for its red wax rind, was sold in Holland without the red protective covering, so our Dutch Edam cheese bought in Holland was pale and without that attraction.

There was a problem, though. Although it was April, spring was later arriving that year than it had been for a long time. We saw some tulips, but only in hothouses, although we took some bulbs back with us and grew them later. On one occasion, there was even a little dusting of snow on the tent flap one morning.

Now, Heather is the sweetest, loveliest, gentlest personality you can imagine. Unless it's cold. She doesn't do too well when it's cold. I had the answer. Cutting our Dutch holiday short, I pointed the MG south and we drove through Belgium and on to Paris. April in Paris! Yes, it really was that good and Heather reverted to her usual sweet self.

Both then and the following year, we stayed at the Bois de Boulogne camping area in Paris. It was the place you met anyone and everyone. We all went there. I was walking back to our tent one day when I heard a voice call my name. I looked and there was Judy Gardiner, one of the girls with whom I had been at university and who was a resident at Crown Street at the same time as me. She and her husband were doing what we were doing. He was working towards qualifications as an orthopaedic surgeon and they were on holiday in Paris.

Another time as we were walking through the camping area, we saw a grey camper van with Australian stickers on it, so we went to say 'G'day.' It turned out that those folk and us had some common acquaintances. Later, David and Sally Roberts Thomson told us that they had just bought a camper van. You guessed it: it was the same van!

Soon after returning to England, two things happened with the MG. One was that some low life pinched the roof rack while it was parked and we were shopping. The other was that it was developing some problem getting into and out of second gear. As we were starting to find it a bit small, and conscious that Andrew was on his way, I traded it on a 1965 Hillman Super Minx station wagon. Sorry, this was the UK – estate car. If I really wanted to be uppity, I would call it a shooting brake. I was thrilled. A car only five years old and with only 44,000 miles on the clock! We bought a station-wagon-length roof rack for it but I took it off and stood it up in the yard at the bungalow in Swindon when we were not actually using it.

The following year, when I was registrar at Harlow, I had four weeks holiday in June and we again went to Europe. We had Andrew by then. He travelled in his carrycot on the back seat and Ian sat beside him. I remember packing the car outside our quarters at Harlow. Time was slipping by and we had to get going as we had some way to drive to get to Harwich or wherever it was that we were catching the hovercraft to Bruges. I had just used the last bit of space in the back of the wagon and was about to close the tailgate and tell Heather to hop in when she came out with yet another cardboard carton of stuff. I honestly don't know how we fitted it in, let alone in time to get to the port. The car was so full on that trip that when I bought a new roll of film we had difficulty finding a place to stow it. Literally.

We saw Bruges, Paris and a good deal of Switzerland, where my aunt was in Geneva. We went to too many places to list but loved the tiny country of Liechtenstein. Then we went to Lindau and stayed with an American architect and his wife whom we had met on the Greek tour on our way to England. He was of German origin and went back from time to time to visit his parents. He happened to be there at the time we were, so that was good.

Lindau is beautiful and we stayed two nights. It has a beautiful ancient tower that didn't seem so beautiful to us once we found out that in days of yore its purpose had been to execute condemned prisoners by locking them in and starving them to death.

We went to Bavaria, where we bought a cuckoo clock in the Black Forest. I think little Ian was a bit afraid a bear might emerge from the forest and eat us. We visited Garmisch Partenkirchen and Baden Baden, and got as far east as Innsbruck. I was surprised at how beautiful the countryside was, and Heather found out how bad her hay fever was as we drove through pine forests.

We didn't go further east. I would have liked to visit Hungary but we didn't really have the time and I wasn't that thrilled about taking a fully loaded car and family into a communist country.

The Short Course and the MRCOG Exam

An organisation in London called the Institute of Obstetrics and Gynaecology put on two full-time courses to prepare for the membership examination. There was the 'long' course, which I think may have been six months, and the 'short' course of two weeks. Doing the short course was part of the tradition, a rite of passage in one's career path while working as a registrar.

The exams, and therefore the courses, were held twice a year. I was enrolled for the January 1972 exam and the preceding short course to prepare for it was in November 1971. My study leave entitlements gave me the time off and paid for the course.

Because Harlow was outside the London suburbs, albeit only by one station, the rules said they would organise accommodation for me to live-in in London for the two weeks of the course. I went home during the weekend in the middle.

The accommodation organised for me was at the Royal College of Surgeons premises at Lincoln's Inn Fields in London. The course venues were several of the most famous hospitals in the world for O&G, such as the Chelsea.

Although London is reasonably spread out, I got up early enough in the mornings to walk to most venues, taking my camera with me. It was just wonderful walking past the numerous historic and beautiful places. Lincoln's Inn Fields itself was worth being at, and at the RCS accommodation I was actually able to take a shower. The lectures did not disappoint, so all in all it was a great fortnight and got the mindset right for the exam.

I have always been nervous at examination time. The MRCOG exam was said to have a fifty per cent failure rate. It was also said that fifty per cent of those who eventually achieved it did so on the first attempt.

Strangely on this occasion, important and significant though this exam may have been, I was for once not nervous. That may have been partly because I was too focused to be nervous. More significantly, the exam at that time was a good, practical exam. I knew that what it was testing me for was to see if I could do the job. As at Harlow I was basically left in charge, doing the job, I realised that if I failed the exam, it would mean that I should not be doing what I knew I was doing satisfactorily every day.

The exam consisted of several written tests, sat for in the big hall at the Royal College of Obstetricians and Gynaecologists premises at 27 Sussex Place, Regent's Park, followed by clinical tests at various hospital venues. You were given a patient to take a history from and examine. Then when the allotted time was up, two examiners came along and asked you questions about her.

There were two explanations if the examiners gave you a hard time. One was that you were very good indeed and they wanted to check just how good. The more common scenario was that you were not good and they wanted to see if it might be possible to pass you.

My examiners seemed very relaxed. My last clinical test, at one of the hospitals, was to be followed by the last of the exams, looking at some pathology at the College. I examined the patient; the examiners asked me what I had found and what I would do. Then one looked at the other and said, 'That's what I would do, wouldn't you?' to which his colleague answered in the affirmative and asked me if I knew my way to the College from there.

That was reassuring and when the examiner quizzing me about pathology specimens at the College looked bored, I knew I was comfortably home, although some of those pathology specimens stretched me a bit more than I would have liked.

Paradoxically, the answers I gave at the last clinical exam make me shudder now. Our knowledge and treatment has advanced so much.

While in London doing the short course and the exam, I met several other Australians doing the same thing. One was a nice chap from Perth called Barry Mendelawitz. Now, my cousin John lived in Perth but I would have sounded stupid asking Barry if he knew him. After all, Perth is a large capital city with one or two million people.

When I got back home and spoke on the phone with John, he asked, 'When you were in England, did you by any chance come across my very close friend Barry Mendelawitz?'

Bad Decisions

Unfortunately, from this happy point onwards, I made a series of bad decisions regarding my career. I can only console myself with the knowledge that if I had my time over again, I would probably make the same mistakes, as I didn't know then what I know now.

King Solomon, in the book of Ecclesiastes in the Bible, chapter 7 verse 8, says, 'The end of a thing is better than its beginning.' As I sit here writing this, I realise how true that is. Now retired, I have all I both need and want. Yes, I made a lot of mistakes along the way but God arranged things so I had a lot of fun, adventures and good times despite so often choosing the wrong path.

I do wonder, however, how much the events at the beginning of this book influenced my life, and in turn the lives of my children and probably grandchildren.

How much did the long ages of anti-Semitism affect the attitudes of my forebears, attitudes that were then passed down from generation to generation? How much was I affected by the traumas of the Holocaust on my parents? How much did those traumas affect the way they brought me up, not to mention the direct effects of those events on me as discussed earlier?

I had actually already made one bad decision. About the time I started on the O&G career path, the MRCOG exam became available in Australia. Thus an alternative to coming to England when I did would have been to work in Australia for the required time, do the exam here, then go to the UK for more experience.

That would have meant that I would not have had the pressure of study on top of a punishing work schedule and in the UK I would have sought a more senior registrar position with better hours, better staffing and in a larger and more prestigious place. And had a little more money behind me. But I was all fired up to go to England.

I had not rushed my time to do the exam, so when I got it, the question was, how much longer should I stay there before coming home? I talked with Rita Harrison, the Australian part-time consultant who sometimes worked with us at Harlow. She said, 'You don't want someone looking over your shoulder now, do you?' That was a nice compliment but, as it turned out, not good advice.

I could then have looked at a registrar job in a bigger place or where the chief was someone prestigious. I could also have worked towards the Royal College of Surgeons Edinburgh Fellowship that would have stood me in good stead. That would also have given me time to settle and mature. It was not until much later that I got feedback that indicated that I really had underrated myself and should have continued on to a more prestigious career path. How much was this lack of confidence influenced by my early life and how much did it influence my career choices?

I have always looked young for my age and trying to go into private specialist practice looking younger than my thirty years was not optimal.

Much as we loved our time in England, Heather and I started to feel a little homesick. To that time, we had always had so little money that the thought of going home to Australia just for a visit didn't enter our heads. So we looked for opportunities at home.

Professor E.V. Mackay in Brisbane showed some interest in my enquiries about a position advertised in his department. Eric Mackay was much liked, was editor of the peer-reviewed *Australian and New Zealand Journal of Obstetrics and Gynaecology* and highly thought of by all.

I might not have been successful in applying for the post but I really should have tried. I didn't because, having spent time in Albury, I thought I preferred the country life to the city teaching hospital environment, and would you believe because Heather and I, both NSW folk, researched Queensland and found that kids started school a year later in Queensland than in NSW and we, wrongly, didn't agree with that. I think in reality I didn't have the self-confidence.

And Rita had said that I didn't need anyone looking over my shoulder. What I have come to realise since is that a huge amount of experience gained very quickly does not quite substitute for time spent.

The clincher, however, was our baby Andrew. He had quite bad eczema. In those days, you still needed smallpox vaccinations travelling overseas.

The only exception for entry into Australia without a smallpox vaccination was if you were under one year old and came from the UK via the USA and over the Pacific Ocean. Smallpox vaccinations are pretty innocuous, except in babies with generalised eczema, when they are dangerous.

So Heather rushed back home with Ian and Andrew, arriving in Sydney the day before Andrew's first birthday. No time to spare! Caused a bit of gossip in the family, though.

I resigned from my registrar post, worked out my notice, packed our possessions and followed six weeks later. Before coming home, I drove our faithful Hillman Super Minx station wagon up the east side of England, across Scotland and down the west side. Was it cold in Scotland! Still, I visited Edinburgh, where Heather's father had been a boy, brought a clan tie back for him and climbed the Scott monument, where he said he had carved his initials as a lad. So had about five thousand other people!

I went as far as Wales, where I left the Hillman with friends who had bought it from us, then drove their old Ford Anglia, the model with the backward-sloping rear window, back to Harlow. They were giving it to friends there. My brother Paul's wife Sue is of English origin and they happened to be in the UK at that time, so Paul drove me to Heathrow and I was on the way home.

Albury Part 2

I have already said that in those days specialists in country towns started there in part-time general practice then in due course got out into full-time specialist practice.

One of the GPs in Albury, Brian Twomey, had asked me to work with him as an assistant in his practice. Brian very kindly diverted his pregnant and gynaecology patients my way but that didn't add up to a lot. I was meant to relieve him of some of his general practice workload. The problem was that Brian was a one-man band. I found out later that he had had a succession of assistants, none of whom had stayed. Certainly he was in solo practice when I was a resident at Albury and first got to know him.

So I had gone from an extraordinarily busy position of authority to sitting around all day twiddling my thumbs. From being in charge of a labour ward to a situation where I observed some of the town's less than competent GP obstetricians (there were also some very good ones) making a mess of what should have been simple issues, but I had no authority to say or do anything about it. It was soul-destroying. At least I was being paid.

There was the occasional funny side. One beautiful sunny Sunday, I was on call for the practice when a lady rang and asked me to see her husband, who was having 'terrible trouble with his haemorrhoids'. As it was Sunday afternoon, I assumed he must have had an acute problem, such as a thrombosed prolapsed haemorrhoid. That's acutely painful but easily fixed, so I asked him to go up to the surgery and I would meet him there.

I arrived to find him already there, pacing up and down awaiting me and obviously not in any distress. When he saw me, he said, 'Doctor, I've had a lot of problems with my haemorrhoids and I was wondering if you could give me a referral to a surgeon to get them fixed?' To which I replied, not wanting to be rude, 'Of course, but not until I examine you first.' I then got the largest and coldest proctoscope I could find!

Wodonga

It obviously wasn't turning out successfully with Brian. I was giving him some weekend and night relief from his solo practice but that was about it. I contemplated going back to England for a more senior registrar post for a while, which of course is where I should have been in the first place. The logistics of that were not going to be easy, though.

There were two group practices in the adjacent Victorian border town of Wodonga. (They didn't speak to each other, at least not if they could help it!) One of them, with senior partners 'Tav' Taverney and John Schlink, had just lost one of their four members, Jack Fitzgerald, as Jack had had a heart attack and had to take it easy. They asked if I could join them, which obviously was a godsend for me. A date for me to start there was decided.

That was fine with Brian. However, I turned up one morning about a week before I was due to finish up there to find Brian, who had an Irish temper, in an absolute fury. I had no idea why. As I soon discovered, it was because I hadn't seen the morning paper as yet.

Unbeknownst to me, the Wodonga practice had put in a commencement of practice notice for me starting with them the following week without telling me or any consideration for the fact that I was still working with Brian.

Thus I started at Wodonga a week earlier than anticipated. I was very sorry that I had left Brian like that, though. He was a lovely man and deserved better but I just wasn't able to get through his anger to explain that I had no idea that the ad was in the paper. Such is life.

My time with the practice, in a two-storey building just by the water tower roundabout, was good. We shared the out of hours and weekends and split the profits evenly. John Schlink's financial contribution was always the lowest but as that was because he saw all the least remunerative patients it didn't matter.

They got me to do much of the minor surgery and most of the O&G. The first operation I did for them was a tonsils and adenoids. I understand this is not so common today but that area was highly allergenic with a lot of asthma and that type of problem. There were numerous sickly underachieving kids who got their life back when we did their Ts and As.

The roster wasn't totally equitable as I did an equal share of the out of hours GP roster and took an equal share of the profits but got called in more frequently if someone needed their appendix out or baby delivered even when I was not rostered on. I let that pass in order to retain their goodwill when my three years with them was up and I went into full-time specialist practice.

The place really was very unsophisticated when it came to specialist practice. The local populace considered a doctor to be a doctor. 'Physician and Surgeon' as the university degrees and brass plaques said. To the locals, a 'doctor' looked after everything between scalp and toenails, inclusive. A 'specialist' was more highly qualified, a 'super doctor'. They had no concept of the different specialist fields.

An example of this was when I was on call for the practice one evening and got called to the Wodonga Hospital casualty where a man had been brought in with a heart attack. Not much usually got done for people with heart attacks and we looked after them in the local hospital. However, this guy was in his forties, not seventies, so I felt he warranted a bit more intensive care. You must have something more seriously wrong if you have a coronary at that age.

I explained all this to him and said I wanted to send him to the Albury Base Hospital under the care of the specialist physician, Dr Bill Stephens. He replied, 'Doctor, if I need a specialist, I would rather Mr Geddes.'

Neil Geddes was a specialist surgeon who had recently begun practice in the area, had sold himself very well and was popular. This heart attack victim had no idea of the difference between a specialist surgeon and a specialist physician. A super doctor was a super doctor, a specialist was after all a specialist. He did go to Albury after a little explanatory chat.

I got no referrals from the other Wodonga practice, not because I was in the opposing practice so much as because they felt they didn't need to refer anyone to any specialist. They could handle everything. They sometimes put pressure on patients. David Nelson, the O&G in Albury, told of a patient who came to him. She was a patient of that practice, was pregnant and wanted David to look after her and deliver her baby. The letter she brought from that GP said, 'Here is Mrs —, who wants you to deliver her baby. I am not referring her.'

At that time, Medicare, or Medibank as it then was, required a specific government-issued referral form with a number that had to be quoted on the account in order for the patient to be able to get a Medicare rebate at specialist rates. This patient had a letter of introduction but no valid referral form.

On another occasion, a patient asked for a referral to a specialist and was told, 'I'll give you a referral if you like, but then never come back to me.'

It was said that the senior partner of that practice had been training to be a surgeon when he had to give that up and come and rescue his alcoholic father's practice. He had a chip on his shoulder and didn't like specialists. The other senior partner was also a brilliantly competent doctor who adopted his older partner's attitudes. The two junior members of that practice, while more than adequately competent but nothing like their older 'general specialist' colleagues, had taken on their attitudes. Apart from that, being a very competent GP was not actually equivalent to specialist training.

Horses and Cattle

Some friends from Heather's childhood were friends with some folk called Maddocks who had a dairy farm not too far from Wodonga and kindly invited us to their place for a meal. This was the type of opportunity I craved, to see what country life really was like.

I was impressed with the science of modern farming, with the way they bulldozed a large trench and filled it with hay which became silage that could be fed to the cattle in time of shortage; or at least that's how I remember it.

The machinery was quite sophisticated. The cows came in to be milked with very little effort. They walked into a milking shed consisting of two rows of stalls arranged obliquely in a herringbone pattern with a pit running the length of the shed in between. All clean and with a concrete floor that got hosed out.

A milking machine hung above each stall. The cows walked in and I helped milk them by attaching the suction ends of the milking hoses to the cows' teats. I think they were washed with an antiseptic solution first. The milking machine did its thing and the cows were released, wandered off and the next lot came in.

While the cows were being milked, they stuck their heads through the bail at the front and contentedly chewed on the hay there. Meanwhile, I was in the pit behind them. As they munched on the hay, recycled hay came out the other end and I got covered in it. I didn't mind. I just loved helping out with the milking. I was happy as a pig in mud, so to speak. I was disappointed that they made me clean up and get changed before we sat down at the table for a meal.

Several of the people we knew had small or large farms and kept cattle and we went and visited and helped. I found I just loved the cattle and working with them.

Murray greys are a very good breed of beef cattle and had originally been developed in north-east Victoria at Thologolong, originally an Angus cattle stud owned by the Sutherland family. The current incumbent was

Peter Sutherland, a man about my age. With Peter's help, advice and encouragement, we bought some cattle and started a small Murray grey stud as a hobby farm. We agisted the cattle on a property owned by friends not too far away.

That whole area is also a very strongly horsey area. A chap called McMaugh had a riding school and I tried it out. I wasn't much good, although I loved the horses, and we had several including some ponies for the kids. Our oldest son Ian was very good and won some junior ribbons at pony club events.

At one point – it must have been 1977 as we were about to have the milestone ten-year graduation reunion – I had a very tall (16½ hands) black thoroughbred gelding. He was a gentle animal to handle but could be a bit of a handful to ride. He was OK if you lunged him adequately before you saddled him and lunged him some more after saddling him but before tightening the girth fully. If you were negligent in any of that, he would buck. But he didn't go wild bucking. On one occasion, I was a bit negligent with the routine and had saddled him inside the stable building, which had low beams. As he bucked, he made sure he didn't hit the beams.

An expert riding teacher lady held a school in Albury that I attended. The riding was very disciplined and quite intensive. I had to cut it short by a day or two to go to Sydney with Heather for the ten-year reunion. After all that disciplined riding exercise, I had such a stiff back that when I had to get up for a leak in the middle of the night I had to wake Heather so she could help me roll out of bed. A big horse is wide and if you abduct your thighs you increase the curve of your lumbar spine. My spine has never been the best.

Wodonga Specialist Practice

I worked my agreed three years with the group practice then went into full-time specialist practice in Wodonga.

The first six months went well. I was getting referrals from my old group practice and from the GPs in the surrounding country towns, with a trickle from Albury where my colleagues dealt with pretty well all the work available there. It was a good start. Of course I neither expected nor got any referrals from the other practice in town.

Then a young fellow, Dr H, became associated with my old practice. It appeared that H had spent one year as an O&G registrar, in Australia, not in the UK with the sort of experience you get there, but one year in Australia, no exams taken or passed. Furthermore, when I was told about his technique in a particular procedure, I worried, as not only was his technique wrong but it indicated a lack of understanding of the basic principles involved. It was a procedure that is safe but has very little margin of safety. That means that if you do it right, it's safe but carelessness can cause disaster. Notwithstanding this, my old colleagues, wanting to keep everything in-house, referred all their O&G to him and my work dried up. I was still getting referrals from the surrounding country GPs but that wasn't enough.

Melbourne was the nearest place with big hospitals and I got a great deal of good advice and support from three senior colleagues there: Ian Mackintosh, former president of the Australian Council of the RCOG; Russell Ferguson, who organised medical students from the Western General Hospital to come to Wodonga; and Professor Norman Beischer from the Mercy Maternity, who welcomed me to postgraduate meetings there.

I rang Norman Beischer to discuss this with him. I felt that if I just tightened my belt and sat it out, the work would come back but I was a bit dispirited at finding myself twiddling my thumbs again, this time without a pay cheque from the practice principal. Norman said no, the days of sitting and waiting were over. If they didn't support me, go elsewhere. So I did.

By now, David Nelson in Albury had a partner, Chris Horsfall. We were all pretty friendly. Years later, Chris and I crossed paths again and caught up. He told me that Dr H had caused numerous disasters and was eventually kicked out. But not before his presence caused me to change career paths again.

The Hawkesbury

Having decided to sell up and leave Albury/Wodonga, the question was 'Where to?'

We found that a doctor who had actually been Heather's GP when she was a child, Dr Peter Degotardi, was now an anaesthetist and told me that they needed an O&G in Windsor. Thus I became not the first specialist to practice in Windsor but the first to be based there.

As Windsor was some twenty or so minutes' drive from the nearest other places, the Nepean Hospital at Penrith or the Blacktown Hospital, to do obstetrics I felt I had to be permanently nearby as there were no junior doctors at Windsor at that time and obstetric emergencies can happen very quickly. If a baby's heart rhythm shows signs of distress, a cord prolapses or someone starts to bleed as heavily as they can after a baby is born, it might be OK if I was in Windsor and the patient in Blacktown or Nepean, as the registrars at the larger hospital could hold the fort until I got there. But if I did any amount of work away, as you will see from the incident of the solicitor's wife and the horse riding, things can happen quickly in obstetrics. So to deliver babies safely at Windsor one had to be close by at all times.

The Hawkesbury area is a very old area of European settlement in Australia. In fact, it is the second oldest after Sydney, older than the settlements in Tasmania. When the first English settled in Sydney Cove, the farming in the area was not good enough to provide food for the infant colony. Accordingly in 1789 under the direction of Governor Arthur Phillip, they sailed their ships north from there and went in the next river mouth, naming it the Hawkesbury River after Baron Hawkesbury. They went as far as it was navigable. European settlers were established there by 1794.

A great flood wiped everything out in 1867, following which Governor Lachlan Macquarie ordered the establishment of five new towns: Windsor, Richmond, Pitt Town, Wilberforce and Castlereagh. These are known to this day as the five Macquarie towns.

At the time our kids were going to school in the late 1970s and 1980s, all that was left of Castlereagh was a hall. The other towns are still present with some very old and historic buildings, the 'Doctors House' where Bill Skinner was incumbent and where I had done a locum in 1969 being one of these.

The TV series *A Country Practice* was filmed in the Hawkesbury.

The Hawkesbury Hospital was the second oldest hospital in Australia, newer only than Sydney Hospital, but until the new hospital was built across the road in 1996, it was the oldest hospital in Australia still on its original site, Sydney Hospital having first been down on Circular Quay before it was moved to Macquarie Street.

At first, the Hawkesbury Hospital did not have any maternity services, so a private midwife converted a house called 'Craignish' into a maternity unit in Ross Street, about a kilometre or less from the main hospital. By the time I went there, this had been acquired by the hospital and was known as the Maternity Unit, or MU, pronounced 'moo'. It was not very satisfactory as we had to wait for an ambulance to take patients to the operating theatre at the main hospital if we needed to do a Caesarean.

Bureaucracy is such that I had to have a severe confrontation with the grossly left wing, doctor-hating chairman of the hospital board to get a demountable building erected on the main hospital site to rehouse maternity services. Despite the obvious sense of this, he publicly accused me of wanting the move only so I could line my pockets. I threatened a defamation action and we eventually got the new demountable building.

The little church at Ebenezer, with some very quaint inscriptions on some of the headstones in its churchyard, is the oldest church in Australia.

I believe St Matthews Church, where Heather and I were parishioners for some time, is the oldest Anglican church in Australia. It was designed by the famous convict architect Francis Greenway and consecrated by Rev. Samuel Marsden. The story went that the foundation stone had to be laid several times as a coin was placed under it and this was repeatedly stolen by the convicts whose labour built the church. Greenway also designed the barracks at the top end of Macquarie Street in Sydney.

When I was young, a couple of wheat silos acted as landmarks at McGrath's Hill on the eastern approach to Windsor. The first wheat in the colony was grown there. There is now a suburban development at McGrath's Hill. Our son Andrew, the one born in Harlow, had his home there with his bride when they first married.

The Richmond RAAF base has its runway taking up the space between the towns of Windsor and Richmond.

We first bought a house in South Windsor, which was nothing flash but had what we wanted. The two horses we had brought with us lived in a paddock at the back and the cattle were agisted on a friend's farm at Grose Vale. We moved there on my thirty-fifth birthday, 5 June 1977.

In 1979 or early 1980 we found twelve acres for sale on the Pitt Town Road, between McGrath's Hill and Pitt Town. Semi-rural acreage and just four kilometres to the hospital. It was on a hill that sloped down to the road – important, as any house site had to be at a certain minimum elevation to be safe from flooding. This is the flood plain of the Hawkesbury River which keeps the low-lying land very fertile but from time to time causes a considerable inconvenience.

We built a house on it and moved in in October 1980. A block of twenty-five acres behind our land became available and we bought that, giving us, taking into account some public land that was only accessible to our property, a total of about forty acres.

It had beautiful views, especially in the early mornings, the light of the sunrise never being the same twice. That aspect has not been there in more recent times since we moved away due to development of a golf course and clubhouse buildings on the other side of Pitt Town Bottoms Road. While we were there, I took numerous photos of the early morning sunrise, no two being the same.

One of Sydney's oldest model flying clubs had its flying field just down from us at Pitt Town Bottoms. I built cattle yards and renovated the historic old convict-built barn. (Sadly that is not there now. The National Trust has apparently not seen fit to heritage list these lovely old relics.)

Heather and I needed a solicitor recently and, our local one here in Queensland having retired, we went back to a solicitor we had known in Richmond. He reminded me of a funny story. We were living in South Windsor still and due to the pressure of work I was getting frustrated at never having the time to go for a ride. One of our two horses was Treble, a stocky little thirteen-hand pony, an excellent stockhorse but otherwise as quiet, well mannered and tractable as you could ask for. If you tied him up somewhere congenial, he would patiently wait for hours if need be.

One Saturday morning I had to go and do my ward rounds but had nothing else planned so I decided to kill two birds with one stone. I saddled Treble up, knowing he wouldn't be spooked by the traffic, and rode him the short distance up the road to the hospital. I tied him up under the shade of a tree in a yard behind the hospital and went to do my ward rounds.

About halfway through the ward round, I got a message (no mobile phones yet) that one of my patients, in fact the wife of this solicitor, had come in in advanced labour and was just about ready to deliver. I raced downstairs to where I had tied Treble up, hopped on his back and cantered him down the road to the MU, where I tied him under another tree in the yard and went in and attended to the childbirth.

My solicitor friend later told me that when he saw me ride up on a horse he thought, 'Strike, I hope he washes his hands!'

The Good

There were a lot of good things about our life in the Hawkesbury over and above the lifestyle of living on a few acres and having animals. That alone was pretty good and a great environment for the kids to grow up in. By now we had three boys: Ian, born in Albury in 1968, Andrew born while we were at Harlow, and now Michael, also born at Albury while I was working in Wodonga.

Although the ground was pretty uneven, the boys and I played cricket beside the house, there was room to run about and ride the horses and somehow we seemed to collect a lot of dogs, as many as five at one point. We had an above-ground swimming pool and the boys learnt to become water safe in that.

At one point, one of the kids, I forget which, had some practical assignment at school that involved rearing day-old chicks. Some time later, without any notice to the parents from the school, he arrived home with a young chook. It turned out to be a rooster who thought he ruled the roost. The dogs were pretty good with him until one day he got just a little too cocky. We didn't eat him, just buried him.

Another time, Michael had a pet goat who was quite congenial and another time Andrew had a duck that was full of character. Our vet was Bob Zammit, who did a regular slot on the TV program *Burke's Backyard*. Bob loved that duck!

The model aircraft national championships were held in the Hawkesbury in 1983, at the Model Club's flying field just down from us and several other suitable venues in the district. Ian had decided he wanted to enter in the junior hand-launched glider competition. Although I have been into model aircraft since I was fourteen, I had no experience with hand-launch gliders, 'chuck gliders', also known as 'chuckies'. This fifteen-year-old kid, using my balsa and tools but otherwise entirely on his own and by himself, researched, designed, built, test flew, redesigned and fine tuned his own little models.

In his first-ever competition, he came first in the Junior Hand Launch Glider and second in the open section.

Rotary

While I was in practice at Windsor, someone thought I would make a good Rotarian and took me along to the local Rotary Club meeting. I duly joined up.

I loved Rotary. It is an organisation that does a lot of good work. One of the guys, Stephen Price, had a mushroom farm and donated the spent mushroom compost. We sold this and raised a lot of money, most of which enabled a local program, Stimulus, to go ahead.

A local woman who had a child with problems had learnt about early intervention and started this group. We provided finance and were able to provide a building for them, not just by using the money to buy building material, but a lot of the fellows pitched in with their labour and trade expertise. Stimulus was one of the pioneering organisations in this field.

A very impressive Rotary program was RYPEN. Rotary is organised in districts and this program sought out promising young business and professional people from one district who, accompanied by a senior Rotarian team leader, visited another district overseas for cultural exchange purposes, the host district of one country sending a team to the other district as well. The local Rotarians provided accommodation and Rotary paid for the fares. The group attended meetings at the various clubs in that Rotary district, the exchangees giving talks on their home towns and professions.

The best-known Rotary exchange program is the student exchange where students from overseas are hosted by members of a Rotary club. The students spent the year with the host club, spending time living with several different Rotarian's families. Thus Heather, the boys and I had living with us as part of the family young people in their late teens, both boys and girls, from South Africa, USA, Finland, Thailand and Japan. There were more students that we personally didn't have the opportunity to host.

Each Rotary club is made up of a representative of each trade or profession in the community. The guys loved it when I described my occupation as a 'delivery man'. What did I deliver? I delivered babies.

Another aspect of Rotary that appealed to me and gave me some balance was that Rotary at that time was a men-only organisation. Like everything else, it has now opened to women. That may be a good thing but I am not aware that the women's service clubs have opened to men. However, I worked with women all the time. I worked with women nurses and midwives, women patients, women office staff. It did no harm to have a bit of male company.

I was president of the Rotary Club of Windsor, District 9690, for 1989–90 but had to give it away a year or two later due to pressure of work.

Flying

All my life I had wanted to learn to fly and had promised myself that 'one day' I would. Of course the 'one day' never seemed to come. I think that, my self-confidence being low, I was actually afraid to fulfil the dream. I didn't really think I could, or was I having difficulty in psychologically giving myself permission?

Every time we drove along the Windsor Road to or from Windsor, I was conscious of the turn off to Schofields Road, with the sign that said, 'To Schofields Aerodrome'. There was a flying club at Schofields.

I did a little work at Baulkham Hills Private Hospital. One Saturday in 1984 as I was driving back home after having been to Baulkham Hills Private, I saw that signpost and realised that the time to do something, anything, is now, or it won't get done. Some of my friends with less of a love affair with aviation than I had learnt to fly. I had been into cattle. I had been into horses but I hadn't learnt to fly. I felt, 'If I'm going to do it, just do it!'

I was concerned about the cost of learning to fly but I thought, 'If I save up for one lesson a month, it may be slow but will be infinitely quicker than what I had done up till now,' which was nothing but dream. Accordingly, I took the plunge, turned left at the intersection and arranged a trial instructional flight.

I was surprised at what a fine aircraft the Piper Warrior, one of Piper's Cherokee series, was. I didn't have a clue where we were, as I wasn't used to seeing the landscape from above like that, but arranged to start my lessons. I was told what books to study and what maps to get.

My instructor at Schofields was Bob Paddock. Bob was very good and put up with me even though some of the time that he was talking to me between flights I nearly fell asleep. (An occupational hazard for obstetricians.) Bob taught me very well but for some reason I just could not master landings. That's important as take-offs are optional but landings are mandatory. Unfortunately, take-offs are much easier.

I could not be sent solo until I could land the aircraft. I had a change of instructor, to Alan Cole at Navair at Bankstown. Alan took me up for a lesson. On the second lesson, he told me to stop completely after we had touched down from a touch and go in the circuit, hopped out and told me to do the next circuit on my own.

Solo, at last! It felt strange but good to have the right-hand seat beside me vacant but, take-offs being no problem, I felt confident as I climbed out. I was so excited that when I found myself catching up on a slower Cessna 152 on the downwind leg of the circuit that my initial reaction was to feel for the brake pedal. I collected my thoughts enough to fly the circuit a bit wider to stay behind him. I didn't have the confidence to throttle back and fly a little slower than I was used to. I didn't want to stall in the circuit.

I felt a bit sorry for Bob. He had actually taught me well and my problem was that I was stuck in a rut. Alan broke the pattern. For a long time afterwards, every time I landed I could hear Bob's voice telling me what to do. If only I could actually have done it with him in the right-hand seat.

I had gone to the Navair Flying School at Bankstown as we had decided to buy an aircraft. What a dream come true for me! Heather's father passed away suddenly and far too young in 1972. He had died without a will, so it took some time for his estate to be finalised but eventually Heather came into a little money. She bought a time-share at Tangalooma, where the family enjoys holidays to this day. She also did something I don't understand with the money and was able to get a sufficient loan to buy a plane.

Jim Hazelton, who was highly respected and much loved in the local aviation community, owned and ran Navair, a flying school and charter service at Bankstown. He had had some financial issues due to problems with the business aspects associated with a Beech King Air so he sold off two of the Piper Warriors he had on line. The deal was that we bought the aircraft and it stayed on line at Navair. They left it on line at the flying school, charging us for the fuel, maintenance and an administrative booking fee for its hire. Thus it earnt its keep and my flying became virtually free.

VH-SWW, Sierra Whisky Whisky, was a very good example of a Piper Warrior. It was fun sometimes flying into Bankstown if one of Schofields' Warriors was also coming in at the same time. It was VH-CWW so the controller at Bankstown tower had to differentiate between 'Cherokee Charlie Whisky Whisky' and 'Cherokee Sierra Whisky Whisky'. Maybe he needed the alcohol after that!

All good things must end sometime and when Jim retired and sold Navair, the new owner did not offer as good a business arrangement. That started my association with Roy Coburn. As we eventually discovered, Roy was what a mutual acquaintance described as 'a likeable rogue'. However, for most of our time with him, the arrangement was mutually very good.

Roy was a LAME, licenced aircraft maintenance engineer, who ran his own business at Bankstown. Roy had a number of aircraft of other owners, such as us, in his hangar. He hangared them for free and rented them out only to experienced pilots, no students, so less stress on the aircraft, for a small booking fee only. In return, he got the business of doing the maintenance. That worked well.

Roy was a character. He had been the aviation adviser to Jack Brabham, the Australian Formula One motor racing champion and had done a lot of things in his time.

Now we probably would have done very well had we kept SWW but I wanted to expand my aviation experience and also get something a bit faster.

For example, flying between Sydney Bankstown and the Gold Coast was four hours planned flight time in the Warrior. In a faster aircraft, such as the Comanche we ended up getting, it is three hours. That's only one hour difference. But the Warrior had an endurance of five hours and it was always wise to land and refuel before you got near the last drop of fuel. So, in case of adverse winds or other problems, it was wise with the Warrior to land somewhere mid-flight such as Port Macquarie or Coffs Harbour and refuel. When you took into account the time taken in the circuit, the time on the ground and the time taking off and getting to altitude again, the elapsed time in the Warrior was close to six hours. The Comanche, three hours. That's not to mention the greater load-carrying capacity of the larger aircraft, not unimportant with a family going on holiday.

The Piper Comanche, in its single or twin engined incarnations, is universally acknowledged as a very good aeroplane. Roy knew and loved them. He found us one for sale at Bankstown, Comanche 260B, VH-AZK.

One of the midwives at Hawkesbury was that rare creature, a male midwife. Jon Johansen is a great guy and apart from being a good midwife was an enthusiastic aviator with quite a few hours in his logbook. Jon joined Heather and me and we combined resources and bought AZK. I can't remember if Jon got his instrument rating on her or already had it. He got his commercial licence on her, though.

The first time we went for a flight in AZK to try her out before purchase, I was at the controls. We had been flying on one of the main tanks and decided to change to one of the auxiliary tanks, which had plenty of fuel. All went well until, about twenty or thirty seconds later, the engine sputtered and stopped. Over rough bush too.

We spend a lot of time in aviation practising for emergencies and deal with a lot of simulated emergencies, but you know they are simulated. You cannot know how you will react in a real emergency until one actually happens. I was pleased that I was immediately into the drill: mixture full-rich, fuel pump on, change tanks back to what you were on before, check the magnetos... Wait a minute, the engine started up again. The Comanche had six tanks and two fuel tankselector valves. In my lack of familiarity with the aircraft, I had accidentally selected the empty tip tank instead of the full auxiliary tank. It took that twenty or thirty seconds for the fuel in the pipes to be used up.

One of the most memorable flights we had was when I had a medical conference in Perth, so Jon and I, with youngest son Michael in the back seat, flew to Perth in her. I have now seen the Bight from low level. It's spectacular.

Another memorable flight was with Bruce Brown as passenger.

Bruce was a wonderful man. During the war, he had been a fighter pilot, initially on Spitfires in the European theatre, then recalled to Australia due to the Japanese threat. He served in PNG flying a P40 Kittyhawk. After the war he was very civic-minded and had served as shire president for the Colo Shire. I got to know him in Rotary, where he was a tireless worker. Despite the evidence of Japanese atrocities Bruce had seen in PNG, he believed today's Japanese to be totally different and did a lot to improve Australian/Japanese relations with sister city programs and such.

Bruce was over the moon when the Australian War Memorial in Canberra located his old P40 and restored it. It is there on display to this day.

It was a great and humbling privilege to take this man for a short flight in AZK. We took her up to altitude and I did a stall. Bruce laughed with delight, saying, 'I haven't done that for over forty years!'

I was still having some difficulties with my landings and mentioned this to Bruce. Having been watching me, he said, 'You were looking out the side as you pulled the nose up when you flared. Look out the front and aim for the end of the runway, keep her flying as long as she'll stay in the air.' Good advice.

You could always come up or down the coast to the entrance to Sydney Harbour at low level below controlled airspace and then request air traffic control for clearance for a flight over the harbour. A beautiful spectacle, especially if you requested an orbit east of the Bridge. Sometimes you had to orbit there anyway while an airliner went by. I took Gordon and Enid Jolly for that flight on one of their visits.

On Australia Day 1988, Australia's Bicentenary, air traffic control anticipated a huge demand and for the day opened a temporary general aviation corridor from Bankstown, over the northern suburbs, down the northern beaches, up the harbour via the heads and back to Bankstown. I did that trip three times that day with various family and friends as passengers. What a sight the harbour was. Wall to wall boats. You could have just about walked across the harbor stepping from deck to deck.

Perhaps the most memorable good landing I had in AZK, after Bruce had given me that advice, was, if I read my logbook right, on 20 December 1991. I was flying from the airstrip at our Tangalooma time-share on Moreton Island to Coolangatta. I had just turned onto final approach when the tower requested me to spend minimum time on the runway as there was an RPT (regular public transport) jet airliner behind me. They don't like having to go around. It's a lot of expensive fuel and upset passengers because some private pilot has been amateurish and baulked their approach. I acknowledged the request, then reconfigured my mind and the final approach for a short field landing.

At Coolangatta there is a taxiway to enter or leave the runway very close to the southern end, from which I was approaching. I touched down right at the southern tip of the runway and turned off onto this taxiway. The airliner captain thanked me via radio, a compliment indeed coming from a professional airline pilot to an amateur private pilot.

Then I missed an opportunity that I have regretted ever since and shall never get again. Under certain conditions, especially some portions of take-off and landing, an aircraft's wing disturbs the air considerably. This is known as wake turbulence. When a small aeroplane is following a large aeroplane closely, the air traffic controller who might give the small plane landing or take-off clearance may well warn, 'Beware wake turbulence' as this can be dangerous to the following aircraft if too close. I missed the opportunity to acknowledge the airline captain's call with, 'Beware wake turbulence.'

Returning to Schofields from Coolangatta the next day was one of the most memorable flights I have ever had. By then I had the instrument rating which enabled me to fly in conditions of poor or no visibility, as in cloud. I never bought an airline ticket once I had that and did not have to worry and keep an eye on the sky in case the weather clouded over if we went away even a short distance for a weekend.

I filed an instrument flight rules (IFR) flight plan from Coolangatta to Schofields. Between Coolangatta and Coffs Harbour all was well. After that, it was in cloud all the way, with embedded thunderstorms that we avoided, and considerable turbulence. My nephew David was with us. He is now a captain on Jetstar with considerable flying experience but maintains to this day that that was the most turbulent flight he has ever been on. And you can't use the autopilot in turbulence, so I was hand flying the bucking aeroplane while flying blind on instruments and calculating flight plan amendments to avoid the thunderstorms. Then I woke up and simply asked flight service to give me a radar vector around the storms. That made life easy; they just told me what heading to hold or turn onto.

We broke visual over the central coast near Gosford. Air traffic control routed me out over the sea, down the northern beaches and via the harbour to Schofields. As we broke visual and went out towards the coast and down the northern beaches, there was the most magnificent sight I have ever seen. We were suspended in space, looking out over the luminous gloom. There were several thunderstorms ringing Sydney out to sea, fortunately well clear of our path. Such magnificent power; black clouds, purple light plus lightning flashes. An awesome display of God's might and majesty.

When we landed in windy, overcast, rainy conditions at Schofields and people asked where we had flown in from, I'm afraid my ego did swell a bit when I nonchalantly said we had come from Coolangatta.

Meanwhile, Jon Johanson retained an interest in the Comanche although he had moved to Darwin. He was the restless kind and having gained his commercial licence and having the instrument rating, he found some flying work and did nursing to supplement his income as needed. He had the dream of building his own aircraft and flying it to the world's largest air show at Oshkosh, Wisconsin, USA. He had chosen a very good kit-built aircraft, an RV4, and commenced construction in Darwin.

Jon had trained as a nurse before it was a university course and found himself at a disadvantage without the university degree. They had a course at Adelaide for the numerous people in that situation so he moved to Adelaide and did that.

In Adelaide he completed the RV4, now registered VH-NOJ. That's Jon spelt backwards. The registration JON was already taken. He did some rather staggering proving flights, including some nonstop Adelaide to Auckland and the like, setting numerous class records before he had even set out for Oshkosh.

He planned a trip to Oshkosh in time for the 1995 air show. As he was going that far, he decided to come home 'the long way round' via the Atlantic, England, Europe and Asia. We, especially Heather, were involved in the home organisation for him.

Well, he made it, becoming only the second person, and the first Australian, to fly solo around the world in an amateur-built aircraft, breaking and setting numerous records along the way.

He did it again the following year, this time east to west against the prevailing winds. Thus he became the first person to fly solo around the world twice. He did it again, going north to south and over both poles.

He ran into some trouble accessing fuel in Antarctica. The Australian government weren't helpful. You'd think they would recognise and support an Australian setting records like Jon was. At least at one point he was named South Australian of the Year.

He now lives quietly outside Adelaide with his wife on a property with his own airstrip, does a little work making accessories for RV aircraft and doing some nursing.

Another aspect of my aviation interest was that I was a member of the Aviation Medicine Society and of the RAAF. I applied for and received recognition by CASA as a designated aviation medical examiner (DAME). CAMS, the Confederation of Australian Motor Sports, canvassed DAMEs to see if they would also do their medicals, so I did that as well.

When I did the trip to America with Andrew at the end of 1988, we bought a Piper Archer, a 180-horsepower version of the Cherokee, the Warrior being 150 or 160hp. We sold that when it arrived and Roy had put it together for us. Heather also went to NZ to pick up a Piper Arrow, a 180hp retractable undercarriage version of the Cherokee. She did the paperwork and the business then flew back in it as crew with Ray Clambach the ferry pilot.

Neither of those aircraft trading exercises was profitable but we did have fun. And how many people can say they have flown NZ to Australia in a single-engine light aircraft?

The RAAF

Peter Degotardi, who asked me to come to Windsor, had been active in the RAAF Specialist Reserve for a long time. He was highly respected and had done a lot in the development of protocols for *med*ical *evac*uations. (Note: *medical evacuations*, medevacs, not medivacs.) Many of the specialists doing sessions at Windsor were also in the RAAF Specialist Reserve.

The Specialist Reserve consists of reservists who are there by virtue of their specialist expertise, whether doctors of various disciplines, lawyers, pharmacists and so on. We had some minimum obligations for how much we did for the service but not as regular as the 'weekend warriors', the Active Reserve.

Peter arranged for me to see Wing Commander (WGCDR) Geoff Nelson, then CO of 3 RAAF Hospital at Richmond. Geoff was a great guy and a competent administrator as CO. He had been a surgeon of some note but was sadly crippled and therefore stuck to a desk job. This was the result of a severe car accident that had happened when Geoff was a little under the weather. I say that not to blemish his memory or upset his descendants but to emphasise that drinking and driving don't mix.

As a result of our meeting, I did regular sessions every fortnight at 3 Hospital and saw patients for them in my rooms when that was more suitable. I applied for entry into the RAAFSR and eventually got there. Peter Degotardi thought the delay might have been because I had been born in Budapest, and Hungary was then still a communist country.

The Specialist Reserve had allocations of each specialist by state. The allocation of O&Gs for NSW was two, a wing commander (lieutenant colonel equivalent in the army or commander in the navy) and a squadron leader (major equivalent in the army or lieutenant commander in the navy).

I was accepted in as a flight lieutenant, FLTLT, the lowest rank for any doctor in the RAAF. The reason for this was because both the WGCDR and SQNLDR slots were allegedly taken. When I checked, I found that the colleague whose name was against the WGCDR allocation had long since been promoted to group captain and used in a different capacity and the one whose name was against the SQNLDR slot was actually Navy Reserve. He was a nice guy who turned out to be a good friend of my old chief Gerald Banwell and brought Gerald out to visit us when he was in Australia.

Both these colleagues were of good standing and happily saw patients for the RAAF when requested but it meant both slots were vacant, I was doing all the work for the RAAF and I was held down at FLTLT level. I tried to point this out to the powers that be but it all fell on deaf ears. It wouldn't surprise me if my requests were counterproductive. Much as I loved the RAAF they are a big and very bureaucratic bureaucracy and many career officers don't like reservists although the service depends heavily on them.

Despite that frustration, I very much enjoyed my time in the RAAF. Apart from the work they sent me, female RAAF members, I saw quite a few wives of RAAF members. These were seen as the usual private or Medicare patients as, unlike the RAF in the UK, the RAAF does not provide medical care for serving members' families.

I attended a week-long reserve officers' familiarisation course at historic Point Cook in Victoria, many postgraduate military medicine weekends at Richmond, 2 aviation medicine courses, one at Point Cook and one at RAAF Base Edinburgh, just north of Adelaide. Later when I was living in Townsville, the RAAF sent me on an early management of severe trauma (EMST) course with military module added, run by the College of Surgeons.

I went for a week on Exercise K95 at RAAF Tindal, near Katherine in the NT and was asked by the RAAF doctor there to go back a little later when there were no exercise activities but I would have the opportunity to see the female RAAF members who appreciated the opportunity to see a gynaecologist despite their remote location. On that occasion, I had the chance to see the spectacularly beautiful Katherine Gorge.

We had to work hard during K95 as we had to deal with the simulated war casualties as well as with the real medical work inherent in such a large exercise.

In the 1980s there was a RAAF base at Butterworth in Malaysia, on the mainland opposite the island of Penang. When RAAF personnel were posted there, as it was out of the country, the RAAF did pick up the tab for their families' medical care. I was jealous of the stories with which my colleagues regaled me of their times there. At first there was no call for me to go but later there was a gynaecologist there who was actually a RAAF member and I went up there for a couple of weeks at a time to give him holiday relief.

All told, I had five trips up there. All wonderful experiences, especially after I had joined Rotary and made up the weekly meetings I missed at home, at the Rotary Club of Butterworth. That got me out from the expat RAAF community and in among the local people, which was great. Not that I didn't enjoy being in the expat community. It was a welcome change for a short time from the very unsatisfactory work situation back home. I went as a FLTLT the first four times but went as SQNLDR for my last trip there in January 1987. I wasn't SQNLDR for very long, the promotion to fill the vacant WGCDR slot coming fairly quickly.

On that last trip, I got away at the weekend for a bus trip to HatYai in Thailand. Although a tourist destination in southern Thailand and frequently visited by the substantial Australian expat RAAF community, hardly anyone spoke or understood English. It was a challenge to order something edible in the dining room.

There were a lot of other attractions around Butterworth and Penang. As I could get married quarters, the two older boys came up and joined me once, and another time Heather was able to come up with the three boys. On another occasion, she rented a car and took the children for a few days up into the very scenic highlands.

On my last attachment there, in January 1987, I was able to get a 1 hour flight in the back seat of a two-seat Mirage jet fighter. Although I had little flying experience, I nevertheless did have my pilot's licence and we owned SWW, so I got to take the controls. The RAAF pilot showed me how to do a roll, then asked if I wanted to do one. The Mirage rolls so quickly and I was having so much fun that I did two.

He showed me how they fly a GCA, 'ground controlled approach'. Very precise! 'If he asks you to change your angle of descent by half a degree, just do it!' Then he gave me a go at it and I did OK.

I got out for a flight at the local civilian flying club and flew over the harbour the day they opened the Penang Bridge. There are now two bridges but the ferry still operates.

On two occasions I was able to take the controls of a Caribou while flying en route and I also flew at the controls of a PC3 Orion. 'The guys in the back looking at their screens don't want to get airsick, so keep it steady!' That was a most interesting flight. Fairly short for what the Orions often did, it was just nine hours! I saw just how fascinating the shipping was in that very busy crossroads of the maritime world.

Once when the Queen was in Australia, she visited RAAF Richmond and Heather and I were invited to a formal presentation of colours and then a garden party with HM. I saw her from a distance. She really is so small. By the time we were able to get to the garden party, HM had already left, much to my disappointment.

The RAAF was involved in quite a few medevacs. Not many were in my field but some were and I retrieved an Australian girl with pregnancy complications from Bougainville, before all their troubles, and another from Lae in PNG and also from Rabaul in New Britain.

I have delivered a baby by Caesarean section and removed an ectopic pregnancy on Lord Howe Island. and on returning from my last trip to Butterworth we diverted first to Chang Mai in Thailand, where an Australian girl had a severe leg injury from a motor scooter accident and we medevacced her back on our scheduled return flight in the C130 Hercules. That was good for me because, instead of being cooped up in a little seat, I was able to spread out in relative comfort at the rear of the aircraft, where the patient was on a litter. I had an easy trip but the nurses worked very hard looking after her. That was my only trip to or from Butterworth in a C130; the others had all been in the ex-Qantas Boeing 707.

Shortly before leaving Windsor, I was presented with the Reserve Forces Decoration, RFD, which is post-nominal. I basically got it because I had been in the RAAF for some time and had done my bit. As I was leaving Richmond, the staff at 3 Hospital presented me with a beautiful large framed photograph of a C130 Hercules in flight, very nicely inscribed.

There was a large army base at Townsville and a somewhat smaller air force base. Military personnel are posted to different places in their careers and will often choose one of them in which to settle once they get out of the service. Townsville is a very congenial place to live, so many ex-RAAF people lived there and I came across many in the community whom I had known and some whom I had delivered at Hawkesbury.

Townsville Hospital is a government institution, so I had military service leave that opened up new possibilities. It was quite difficult, and, frankly, expensive, for me to take two weeks off at a time to go to Butterworth. Besides, Butterworth was no longer an option as the RAAF base there, inherited from the British RAF, had in turn been passed on to the RMAF, the Royal Malaysian Air Force, although I believe a P3 Orion remained there on rotation.

As I could take military service leave with no concerns for my practice or the cost of a locum, I was able to spend two deployments of a fortnight each at Bougainville, a month at Timor Leste and later another fortnight there.

I got the ASM, the Australian Service Medal, for my time in Bougainville and the AASM, the Australian Active Service Medal, for the time in Timor, as Timor was at that time declared a warlike zone.

Paradoxically, Bougainville was scarier. For a start, in Timor we were armed so no one messed with us and by the time I was there, things were much more settled. In Bougainville, our role was as a peace monitoring group. Monitoring, not keeping, thus we were unarmed.

The fighting in Bougainville had died down by then and the Bougainvillean people are lovely gentle folk. But Bougainville is a province of PNG and some PNG provinces had alcohol prohibition, like in the US in the 1920s. Bougainville was one. So the people, being innovative, produced their own. One of the most potent local brews was 'jungle juice' and heaven only knows what it contained. Let's just say that people with a skinful of that were not so peaceful. I had to patch up a few with quite serious machete wounds. Also one lad whose arm had been badly hurt by a grass knife, a 'payback' attempt. Lucky for him that it wasn't a machete; that would have taken his arm off.

The medical facility at Timor was very well equipped and staffed with specialist intensivist, anaesthetist and two surgeons as well as the ADF doctors and nursing staff.

At Bougainville, apart from the service nursing staff and an ADF doctor, there was a specialist anaesthetist and a surgeon. (I was deployed as surgeon; the real surgeons had to handle any obstetrics and gynaecology when it was their turn.)

At Timor, our facility was at Dili. The airport was at Dili and there were planes to and from Darwin all the time and we could phone Darwin if need be.

At Bougainville, there was a C130 Hercules once a week from Townsville and we were almost an hour's drive to the airfield. Altogether much more isolated and with fewer facilities and personnel.

Bougainville was in many ways a sad reminder of the devastation of war. I delivered a baby by Caesarean for a lovely couple who were schoolteachers, but the schools had been closed for ten years. That would be the entire education time for a whole generation.

As we drove from the airfield at Kieta to the camp in the old ore loading shed at Loloho, on roads that had not been repaired in a decade, we passed by the town of Arawa, from where I had some years before retrieved an Australian girl with pregnancy complications.

The formerly large and prosperous town was a ghost town just starting to be reinhabited. The hospital, once the largest in the Pacific Islands, had been burnt down. Later, my anaesthetist colleague and I performed the first, albeit minor, surgery there, although it was only in an outbuilding. More buildings of the hospital were in use on my second deployment there the following year.

We were housed in two-person tents erected in the shelter of the old copper ore storage shed at the port of Loloho. The bay was beautiful but you couldn't eat fish caught in it due to the heavy metal contamination. We played a fun game of cricket with a large ball in the yard at the back of the camp shed. The concrete rendered wall was pockmarked where bullets had hit it. That's where they had lined up people and executed them by firing squad.

My last contact with the RAAF was when I did a week's relief manning at the small medical facility at the RAAF Base at Townsville just before my sixty-fifth birthday. I had the opportunity to requalify on the pistol and, much to my pleasant surprise, scored in the top range. A nice farewell as, although I consider myself usually a good shot, I had done abysmally for some reason the last time I shot the Steyr rifle.

The CRA, compulsory retiring age, had been fifty-five and I had been extended to what I believed was the maximum, sixty, shortly after I arrived at Townsville. At the time of my first deployment to Timor, I was due to turn sixty. Indeed, I had my sixtieth birthday during that deployment. That was possible because they said the rules had changed and they could extend me a further three years. I put in my application and found that they had extended me to age sixty-five!

At first I thought that was an administrative error, but no, it was for real. When I turned sixty-five, they again offered me an extension but I declined. They weren't going to deploy me at that age and, much as I had enjoyed it, and got far more out of it than I had put in, it was time.

The Bad

All the good things in the previous chapters were going on concurrently with my work situation. They were merely the background to the work. They were all good but the work had to be acceptable, both in the volume being manageable and the remuneration being reasonable.

Before we went to the Hawkesbury, I did my research. I especially looked at the population:, was it enough to support an O&G, what were the growth predictions?

I knew I would be the first O&G to be based there and that that would take the local doctors and population some time to get used to. I was looking at making a start and then working to make the potential grow into reality.

For almost two years, I was the sole obstetrician there. As pregnant women can come into labour at any time and as there are often situations in which time, measured in minutes or seconds, is of the essence (for example, a prolapsed cord or a severe post partum haemorrhage), I felt that I had to be physically present in the area except for the rare occasion I got a locum, who got paid more than I took in, if a locum could be found. The nearest other hospitals were Nepean and Blacktown, both twenty to thirty minutes away.

I can remember very often being so physically exhausted I could hardly clamber into bed, only to have the phone ring and then be out in the middle of the night with someone's life literally in my hands. But I still had to work the next day.

Rural O&G practice has its advantages apart from the pleasures of the rural lifestyle. One is that one has a captive market, so to speak. In a country town, people who choose to get their medical care elsewhere pay for it with long distances to travel, so are motivated to use local services where possible.

The two major disadvantages of rural practice are the isolation and the fact that, as there are no large hospitals, all patients get their treatment directly from their well qualified doctor of choice.

Thus in the country, patients who would be seen as public patients in a hospital clinic in the city are seen in one's rooms or surgery. The remuneration for these patients is much less than for a private patient but the cost of seeing them, the cost of running the rooms, is the same.

In the Hawkesbury, if I was to provide a safe service, I had to be tied down there. Unlike in a true rural situation, though, the patients weren't. They could and did take themselves off to the fashionable doctors in the fashionable and much less run-down hospitals not too far for them to travel.

A lady in a letter to the editor of the local paper, in extolling the wonderful local lifestyle, quite openly said that they could go to their fashionable doctors in fashionable hospitals happy in the knowledge that there were 'excellent' doctors available locally if they had an urgent problem.

When I began practice there I made a good enough start and got a reasonable number of private patients although many of the recent arrivals from the newer more upmarket areas still went elsewhere. However, I knew I had to start somewhere, so I plodded on. As time went by, the proportion of private patients decreased to very little.

Among the other issues was the very poor behaviour of a number of my colleagues. There were several incidents when I should have told them what they could do and resigned on the spot. I didn't.

The most pivotal issue was that things could not improve until we had a bigger, better equipped and better staffed hospital. Such a hospital would increase the number of patients being treated locally, thus justifying better junior staffing levels and better equipment. The system had to change but could not until we had the new hospital.

The hospital had actually been earmarked for rebuilding for I believe around fifty years. The governments of the day, of either colour, kept telling us that as soon as a hospital somewhere else was finished, we would be next cab off the rank. 'Once we finish — hospital, we'll do Hawkesbury.' This carrot was constantly dangled before us and we never caught up with the carrot. The trouble was that Hawkesbury was a safe Liberal seat.

An unfortunate corollary to the hospital being small was that it had only one operating theatre. Thus if an emergency in some other surgical discipline came in, such as a serious head injury or whatever, then my operating list got cancelled.

Again, I was fool enough to work on a 'fee for service' basis. So if I did an operation for a public patient, the hospital remunerated me to the level of the Medicare rebate for that item number. At seventy-five per cent of the so-called 'schedule fee', it was considerably less than a private fee. Same work for me, though. I didn't sit and read the *Times* while the registrar operated.

The real problem with this system was that if my case got bumped, having performed no procedure, I was not paid. Had I arranged to be paid on a sessional basis, then I would have been paid for a booked session unless adequate notice of cancellation had been given. However, I could not have survived on the sessional remuneration. Add to that, that although so much of my work (ninety-five per cent at the end) was public, which is the hospital's legal responsibility, we had to pay for our own very expensive indemnity insurance.

As the hospital was small with limited resources and no obstetric resident staff, I was the bunny getting up in the middle of the night to put in IVs, sew up women after childbirth and so on, but if a case truly requiring specialist care came along it was likely that the small hospital would not have the facilities to cope and the patient would have to be transferred to a more major centre.

I was exhausting myself on the work that was done by the resident when I was young and having to send away cases requiring a specialist's expertise.

So why did I put up with it so long? The short answer is that I shouldn't have. There were I believe three reasons.

The first is that, as I alluded to in the drinks incident at Ian's birth, while I was very self-assured in my work as I was on familiar ground, I was otherwise naive and non-assertive and let myself get pushed around. I should add that most of the time I was so physically and mentally exhausted that, especially being unused to that degree of bad behaviour, I was in no fit state to respond correctly. To what extent my ability and confidence to handle the situation was directly or indirectly affected by my heritage and background, who can say?

The second is that I knew things could not improve until the new hospital was built. Like others, I chased the carrot before me, for about seventeen years!

Lastly, and most significantly, I loved the lifestyle. Not just all that has been described so far but also I was a part of the community. If I took a moment between patients to duck up to the shops, I would invariably bump into one or two people I knew.

It was the '*Nil batardi carborundum*' attitude. 'Don't let the b—s grind you down.' If circumstances were to prevent me staying there, so be it, but I wasn't going to let go of my dream, either of lifestyle or of my vision of what could be achieved at the hospital, because of the behaviour of those b—s.

I was wrong.

Disaster

We recognised that I was working too hard but I wanted to stay there. One answer was to find some other income source than my medicine so we could have a reasonable living without being dependent on my profession. I think that was a wrong decision. Medicine should be remunerative enough to support a reasonable lifestyle. If a practice doesn't, despite keeping you busy, then there are inherent problems. Go elsewhere. But...

We were offered an agency for some motor vehicle accessories. I knew enough about cars and enough of the physics involved to know that these gadgets, attached to the exhaust pipe, should work. And they did. I used them on our cars and felt a noticeable increase in power and in fuel economy. The trouble is, they didn't sell. There is more to making money from some gadget than knowing that it works. Doctors know medicine but most good doctors are hopeless business people. We were easy prey for the con artists who sold us this opportunity.

So there we were. I was approaching fifty, burnt out and broke. We had built up a small real estate portfolio and sold that. The plane went.

In retrospect, there was at least one property we should have kept. We were desperate and panicking. However, we managed to avoid going bankrupt. That might have been the easier option but it didn't appeal.

The cattle had long since gone. I couldn't keep up with the work. When I awarded myself the DNF (Diploma of Nocturnal Farming), I felt we should sell them. Sometimes I would get home at nine p.m. after a long day and have to get the ladder, go up to the loft and get a couple of bales of hay for the cattle in the yard. Enough was enough and they had to go. We had had them for ten years, 1974–1984.

I knew that despite our hard times God still cared and was with us through them. Without that knowledge, I don't know where I would have been.

Goodbye Windsor

I knew that things at Windsor would not get better until we reorganised the way we provided the service and that that was impossible until we had a new hospital.

Hallelujah! A new hospital was announced! It was to be built on the vacant land opposite the old one. We attended many planning meetings and the government spent $6 million on planning and preparatory earthworks.

Then they pulled the plug. Sorry, we don't have the money to proceed. Six million down the gurgler just like that! But how long had it taken before they spent a couple of thousand or less on a foetal heart rate monitor to keep the technology in the labour ward up to date? Or bought a laparoscope instead of me continuing to use my own personal one? Can't buy today's equipment but can waste six million on a project we haven't the foresight to see we can't finish. Grrrr!

Not long after that, the Uniting Church, which has a health care arm, offered to build a new hospital as a private, not for profit, venture to provide services to both public and private patients.

Great idea! Let's do it! But wait, if we do that, we shouldn't just tell them to go ahead, we should put it out to tender.

They did. The only other party to tender was Catholic Health Care.

Actually, I think they may have asked the Catholics to tender.

The Catholics provide a lot of health care services and are proven and experienced in this field, but so are the Uniting Church. We are talking about public hospital services here, which uninsured patients may not have a choice about.

The problems arise with family planning services such as prescriptions for the pill and sterilisation operations. These are against Catholic beliefs. That is not a problem with a Catholic private hospital. It is a problem when we are talking about a public hospital that should offer these services.

The Catholics came to the party, which didn't impress me as, while I don't share their beliefs, I do feel they compromised their principles.

I could not help wondering. The Uniting Church had thought of and made the offer yet the Catholic Church were invited in and, despite the incompatibility of the Catholic faith with the family planning requirements of a public hospital, won the contract.

A friend and colleague, who was also into local politics, sat on the committee that decided all this and told me it was all above board, but I can't help wondering.

So it was back to the drawing board. Attending numerous planning meetings again to replan the whole thing. The perfectly good plans we had formulated earlier were not going to be good enough, we had to replan from scratch and the earthwork foundations had to be bulldozed and rebuilt.

So there was the new hospital. Did it help? Far from it. The system did not change, so what the new hospital did by attracting more of the local people to go there instead of to other hospitals merely increased the workload and magnified the problem.

I tried to cope as long as I could. I remember standing in the front paddock of our beloved twelve acres watering some trees I had planted and asking, begging, God not to take this away from me. I was in the position that, if things were quiet I worried where our next dollar was coming from as I was on a 'modified fee for service' contract, and if it was busy I wondered how I could physically cope. By now I was fifty-four.

I remember coming home after a busy evening at the hospital, good for the bank balance but nearly killing me. I said to Heather, 'I can't keep doing this. We're going to have to leave.' To which she said, 'I've been trying to tell you that for years.'

I wrote to the new CEO of the new hospital outlining my problems and offering some solutions. He rang me and invited me to lunch to discuss it. He was one of those South Africans who make an art form of being extremely rude in an extremely polite manner. He told me that they were not interested in my suggestions as 'We think you'll never be satisfied.'

I had started the full-time obstetric service at Hawkesbury, providing it single-handed, 24/7, for a couple of years before anyone else came, then putting up with a lot of rubbish because I really wanted to see that hospital become something. I had worked myself into the ground for that place for a few months short of two decades, and all this glib, slick-suited Johnny-come-lately could do was offer me a sandwich and an insult.

I was furious, although I hope I didn't show it, as I didn't want to give him the satisfaction. I didn't resign on the spot, although I felt like it, but went away, considered it carefully and wrote my letter of resignation. And sent it.

The CEO rang me later to ask what was this he had heard on the grapevine that I was leaving? He claimed he had not received my letter. I told him that was his problem, I was not staying later than the date in my letter and if he felt I should give more notice, then I would take the time as sick leave.

On Friday 29 November 1996, our thirty-first wedding anniversary, I was called out of the church where we were attending a friend's wedding to attend a public delivery at Hawkesbury. I made sure all was well and walked out. I did not look back and have never set foot there since.

Postscript

A little after starting at Townsville, I heard that they had appointed a new O&G, Dr G.R., at Windsor to replace me. I rang him, as I would have thought that someone applying for the position would have spoken to the previous incumbent. He told me that they didn't know where I was. Obvious nonsense. It was with mixed feelings that I later learnt he was the infamous 'butcher of B—' since deregistered and jailed. His appointment, considering what was known about him even then, indicates gross incompetence on the part of the hospital board.

Townsville

When I realised that the situation at Windsor was untenable, I had to decide what to do. At fifty-four and burnt-out, I didn't feel like starting a new practice somewhere else and I wasn't sure what other private practice opportunities may be available.

I had heard that Queensland offered salaried staff specialist positions and this seemed a good solution. At that time, staff specialist positions were not really the norm in NSW. There were a few but they were mainly positions new specialists would take for a while until they were known and could start private practice. In Queensland, they were the norm, although there were plenty of colleagues in private practice.

Alex Crandon was a good friend who had been on the staff at Westmead as a gynaecological oncologist, a women's cancer specialist. Some time back, he had accepted a position as the inaugural professor of gynaecological oncology in Queensland. Although based in Brisbane, his responsibility covered the whole state.

I rang him and said, 'Alex, you've got your finger on the pulse of Queensland. What's available in the staff specialist line?' Alex thought I had had a gutful of the antics of my colleague, the other O&G at Windsor. It pleased me to know that my issues were not just imagined but obvious to others. Later, one of my RAAF colleagues said, 'You were not treated well at Windsor.' That's some comfort.

Alex said, 'At the moment, there's only Townsville.' To which I'm afraid I replied, 'Where's Townsville?' He told me, more or less.

I researched it and all I heard was good. That later turned out to be true. Although tropical, the climate was said to be among the best in Australia. My air force friends who had had postings there spoke very highly of it. Remote, yes, but large enough and remote enough to warrant its own cultural and other amenities. Our accountant was very pleased with the financial aspects of the contract, including the provision of medico-legal indemnity insurance for all work done at the hospital or on the hospital's behalf.

So Heather and I were flown up on the October long weekend, 1996, to have a look and an interview. We went up on the Saturday and the interview was the next day. What I remember most is the deputy director of medical services, a nice guy whose name I can't remember, trying to show me the beauty spots of Townsville, which actually are worth seeing. But I was dead on my feet, my usual state by then in Windsor, and all I wanted to do was to fall into bed.

The interview was the next day. On the interview panel was Dr Chris Kennedy; a very able administrator who I later learnt had been brought in to solve the very severe problems that had recently occurred in Townsville. Now that we are all retired, Chris has turned up as a neighbour here where we live on Bribie Island! Chris had headhunted an old classmate of his from Adelaide, Eric Green, as director of O&G. That interview was my first meeting with Eric.

At any rate, I got offered the job and took it.

Townsville was not looking its best as it had not rained for three years, but not only had people I trusted commended it to us, but as Heather said, the salary and conditions were good enough for us to stick it out for three years if we really didn't like it. (They paid our removal costs but we would have to refund the money if we didn't stay three years.)

I then discovered the reason why they were so desperate to have me. The previous administration had so upset our predecessors in the O&G department that they resigned en masse. Eric had been appointed as director but was not taking up the position until another colleague (me) had been appointed as the College would withdraw recognition of the registrar training posts if there were not two fellows of the College on staff, so my appointment was critical. Such a department cannot be run without good quality trainee registrars.

This whole thing was a serious mess as there are only three neonatal intensive care units (NICUs) in Queensland, two in Brisbane, the third in Townsville. Everything from north of Rockhampton to the Northern Territory border and the Gulf, right to the tip of Cape York, even PNG, was our responsibility.

A NICU is dependent on a functioning high-level obstetrics department for obvious reasons. If a pregnant woman has problems with the baby she is carrying, that baby is best transferred to the vicinity of the NICU in Mum's tummy and delivered where the NICU is. All staff obstetricians resigning at once was a problem.

Furthermore, Eric's predecessor, the former director of O&G, while actually a nice guy once you got to know him, and very highly regarded in the army, where he was a lieutenant colonel reservist, had managed to upset everyone, civilians at least, from our colleagues in private practice in Townsville to our fellow staff specialists in other disciplines.

Eric totally reorganised the department into an efficient model in which we worked well. He also worked very hard to rebuild bridges between us and our private practice colleagues and other hospital consultants. It worked.

As I had been appointed, due to start at Townsville on 23 December 1996, Eric was always on the phone to me at Windsor, before either of us started, to discuss various issues about the department with me. He actually arrived at Townsville two weeks after I did.

Two other colleagues were appointed. Ajay Rane, who was working in England, was flown out for an interview by the hospital. He was flown to Sydney and put up in a hotel there, where Eric, who had been flown to Sydney for the occasion, and I interviewed him. Ajay is a great guy, larger than life, a lot of fun and brilliant. He is now a urogynaecologist of world standing and professor at James Cook University.

Shortly after we started at Townsville, we were joined by David Watson. David's forte is materno-foetal medicine and he is brilliant at that, as well as being a good all-rounder and thoroughly nice guy.

Others joined the department in due course.

I started at Townsville just before Christmas 1996 but Heather had to go back, pack, sell the house and so on, all of which took time. Meanwhile, the hospital provided me with some accommodation until I was able to find some to rent for myself. They then gave rental assistance for a time.

While Heather was still 'down south' and I was in one of the hospital-provided apartments, one that was often used for registrars, Eric and his wife Lynne invited me for dinner one Saturday. As I arrived, Eric asked me how I was, to which I answered, 'Wistful.'

While I had still been in bed that morning, but late enough for the sun to be well up, there was a knock at the door. I pulled on a dressing gown to see who it was. There on the doorstep was a very inebriated young lady who was rather unsteadily looking for someone who I presume was the previous occupant of that apartment. Although I realised it might not have been quite proper, in view of her condition I asked her if she was all right and did she want to come in for a while? She declined and tottered off very shakily in her stiletto heels. I thought, 'I hope she isn't driving,' and moments later heard a car start up.

The department blossomed under Eric's leadership. Word about it got around among the trainee registrars and we found ourselves getting a top bunch in very short order.

Unlike Windsor, if ever any of us had a problem or difficult case, we shared it, talked about it between us. Quite the opposite to Windsor, where you kept yourself to yourself to minimise the opportunities for backstabbing. This was so much better a work environment, and better for the quality of care delivered to the patient.

One incident that occurred shortly after our arrival buoyed me up no end. Shortly before leaving Windsor I had a patient by the name of Mitchell who developed a very serious complication of pregnancy known by the acronym HELLP syndrome. My physician, anaesthetist and paediatric colleagues all felt that this was too much to deal with at Windsor, so she got transferred out. A correct decision but frustrating. No sooner had we started at Townsville than another lady called Mitchell, with HELLP syndrome, was transferred to Townsville under my care from an outlying hospital. That kind of pleased me. A good start.

Under Eric's leadership, we took medical students on rotation for the Northern Clinical School of the University of Queensland. Associated with this we were given academic appointments as senior lecturers in obstetrics and gynaecology at the University of Queensland. I also got to be an examiner in UQ's medical course final examination on one occasion and had developed a series of tutorials with accompanying lecture notes for the students on their rotation through our department.

One of the things I really wanted to teach the students and junior doctors was to think and use lab and imaging tests sensibly and not in lieu of using their brains, as this could delay necessary, even urgent, treatment. An example was when the resident told me that a woman had come in, pale as a sheet and in shock with a tender, rigid abdomen. He had correctly diagnosed a ruptured ectopic pregnancy, which caused internal bleeding, which can be life-threatening. He told me that he had therefore organised an immediate ultrasound. I intercepted the patient on the way to the ultrasound and organised for her to go immediately to surgery. Apart from not telling us anything we didn't already know and causing dangerous delay, the ultrasound would have beeen extremely uncomfortable for the patient.

Other colleagues have had similar experiences.

I also found that, once they graduated, intelligent medical students seemed to operate on a set of conditioned reflexes. For example, symptom or sign A indicates test B, indicates treatment C. I tried to drum it into them that they must not stop thinking just because they had the letters after their name.

It always made me feel proud to see our students and junior doctors do well subsequently. One of them did anaesthetics and at the time I left was on the staff at Townsville. When Heather and I were recently referred to an eye specialist, it turned out that he had been one of our medical students at Townsville and remembered the tutorials I had given.

A few years after we started, a new medical school was opened at James Cook University at Townsville so we swapped our affiliation from UQ to JCU.

Kirwan Hospital to the Townsville Hospital

We started our time at Townsville at what was then the Kirwan Hospital for Women. The work we did there was great but the building left a bit to be desired, although it was incomparably better than Hawkesbury before the rebuild.

Way back when Jo Bjelke-Petersen was premier, it was recognised that Townsville's population was, like everywhere else, shifting west. The Townsville General Hospital was in the middle of town, so Jo told the people he would build them a hospital in the western suburbs.

What he actually did was move the O&G, neonatal and, I think, psychiatric departments to a new hospital building in the western suburb of Kirwan. My understanding is that this was actually to make room for the new radiation oncology building beside the General Hospital. This separated us from our colleagues in other disciplines. We had our own operating theatre but had to have a dedicated anaesthetist with us at all times.

Worst of all, ambulance crews are obliged to take casualties to the nearest public hospital. As Kirwan was designated as a public hospital, it meant that people picked up by the ambulance for things like heart attacks, car accidents and so on had to be taken there. We then had to see them and send them on to the General Hospital, thus delaying their treatment and inconveniencing both the ambulance officers and us.

That was not to be forever, though, as a new hospital was to be built, combining the services of both the Townsville General and Kirwan hospitals on a new site in Douglas, on the university campus and about halfway between the centre of town and Kirwan.

It was déjà vu all over again as I once more attended planning meetings, now for the third time. One big difference was that as these meetings were in office hours, it was time for which we were paid. A somewhat fairer arrangement.

We moved into the Townsville Hospital, TTH, on 8 October 2000.

After all the hassles, backstabbing, undermining, power plays and often thankless work and toil at the Hawkesbury, I was a consultant at a university teaching hospital, had an academic appointment as senior lecturer at a university medical school and led up my team of consultant, registrar, resident and medical student.

I had become interested in menopausal medicine, a much underrated and poorly practised branch of medical care. I had joined the Australasian Menopause Society before I had left Windsor, attended conferences and was for a year on the committee of the society. I ran the only dedicated menopause clinic in Queensland outside the southeast corner of the state.

My registrars and I did some research and I also worked with the ultrasound department at Townsville to develop an ultrasound technique of examining the lining of the womb or endometrium. Two papers with the results of some of our research were published in the *Australian and New Zealand Journal of Obstetrics and Gynaecology* and one of my registrars also wrote a paper on the ultrasound, which won her a trip with her husband to a conference in Budapest.

I developed an interest in colposcopy, examination of the cervix to check it out when the pap smear showed a possible problem, and I became a College-accredited assessor of registrar trainees' competence at this as part of their membership training. My registrar and I had a poster presentation on a technique for colposcopic treatment accepted at the international meeting of the British Royal College of O&G in Montreal in 2008. I also presented a paper on the ultrasound topic at that conference.

After three years at Townsville, I had become eligible for overseas study leave. Heather and I had done virtually no travel since our return from England in 1972 but now had the opportunity. The cost to us was her fare as mine was paid for by the study leave entitlements and it costs no extra for two in a hotel room than for one.

I found the study aspect very useful and chose those places to visit where I particularly wanted to go. We went back to Budapest in 2000. I had not been there since leaving as a child in 1948. We visited New York, where our son Ian lives, and made many friends, professional and otherwise.

We went to overseas conferences and revisited the beautiful areas of England where I had worked. I went back to Harlow, where I had been a registrar. It was much different by then. We visited my old chiefs and other friends we had made years before.

Ecclesiastes chapter 7, verse 8 again: 'For the end of a thing is better than its beginning.' Thank you, Lord.

In Queensland, the title 'senior specialist' does not come automatically as time elapses and one ages. One can either be appointed to such a post or, alternatively, one can earn it.

I had not been appointed as a senior staff specialist, so had to earn it. I applied several years running and eventually got there. With that appellation came kudos and a top of the line car instead of the base model. In my case, Ford Fairmont Ghia instead of base model Falcon. No in-betweens.

Apart from work, we felt God was very good to us. When we had the financial disaster, we thought we would never own our own house again, but we did.

I also bought a small plane, a Jodel D150, from a friend who had built it then developed heart problems and could no longer fly. It was a very good aircraft and a lot of fun. It had been beautifully built but the covering was not in good shape. In 2006, I took long service leave and used the opportunity to disassemble, strip, re-cover and repaint the aircraft under the watchful eye of my friend Denis Beahan, who had an aircraft maintenance facility at Charters Towers.

Bribie Island, Locums and Retirement

All good things must end sometime, though. By 2007, the year I turned sixty-five, I was doing my work just fine but did not have any energy left when I got home at the end of the day. I thought that was due to the inexorable passage of time bringing older age with it. In retrospect, there may well also have been the beginnings of the health problems that were soon to manifest themselves.

I resigned and agreed that I would leave at the end of the first week of January 2008, as that was when the old contingent of registrars and residents left and the new ones came. Anticipating this, Heather and I had pondered whether we would stay in Townsville or go elsewhere when I retired. We had pretty well decided to stay in Townsville, as we were very happy there.

However, our son Andrew and his family used to come up around Christmas or New Year and have a holiday with us. One time that they did this, after they had gone home I realised how much I missed them.

Townsville is a long way from anywhere. To drive to Sydney is twenty-four hours on the road, two and a half to three days' drive. Although there is a direct flight to Sydney every day, the cheap seats get booked up fast.

We decided to find somewhere closer to Sydney but did not want to move back to Sydney itself, even if we could have afforded it. After some Internet research, we checked out Bribie Island, an outer northern suburb of Brisbane, bought a place virtually as soon as we saw it and have been happy ever since.

There are several planes each hour between Brisbane and Sydney and I have several times got in my car at home in the morning and got out at Andrew's place in the evening, although I'm too old for that now.

At first, Andrew and family were not happy with us as they loved coming up to Townsville but they don't complain about the attractions of Bribie now they have got to know it.

Although I had given up full-time work, I was not ready to stop altogether yet. Partly because I wanted to keep working a little longer and partly because we were not quite there yet financially.

I therefore worked part-time doing locums, relieving for other doctors when they were away. This was great. Others may buy a four-wheel drive and caravan and do the grey nomad thing. I saw Australia by working all over it, from Darwin in the north, Port Hedland and Perth in the west, Launceston in the south, Mt Isa, Alice Springs, Goulburn, Taree, Bundaberg, Wagga Wagga. Even a short stint at the Mater in Brisbane. Redcliffe and Caboolture closer to home.

I became a regular at many of these places. I did a couple of longterm locums at Caboolture and finished my career working half-time, then quarter-time, at Wagga.

Heather joined me some of the time. She herself was working in fairly high level medical practice management positions. She sorted things out, administratively speaking, at Thursday Island. As I went up there a couple of times to be with her, I saw TI as well and she later did the same for a new superclinic in the western Victorian town of Portland.

I had a delightful experience relieving at Taree one time. I arrived in labour ward on the Friday morning to see what there was for me. The midwife told me there was a lady waiting for her labour to be induced so I went to check her out and discovered she had a breech presentation. I told her that yes, she would have her baby that day but it would be best delivered by Caesarean. No problem and we did it later that day.

I went to check on her in my ward round in the usual way the next morning. Her mother was with her and immediately greeted me. 'Hello, Dr Kraus.' How did she know my name? It turned out that when I first was at Windsor she had been a midwife there. To my shame, I did not remember her – admittedly it was over thirty years previously. To add to my embarrassment at not recognising her, when she herself had fallen pregnant I had looked after her and delivered her baby, the very same one whose baby I had just delivered by Caesarean. What a small world.

The story of the last hysterectomy I ever did is worth telling as it illustrates several of the challenging issues of remote and rural medicine. Issues associated with remote locations, huge distances and sparse and often 'at risk' populations.

Hysterectomy, removal of the uterus (womb), was a common gynaecological operation usually done to cure intractable heavy menstrual bleeding, or sometimes because the uterus had become enlarged by noncancerous growths of its muscle tissue, a condition known as fibroids. It is less common today as new treatments have been developed. An emergency hysterectomy is rare and usually associated with otherwise uncontrollable bleeding at Caesarean or, more rarely, other forms of childbirth.

I was doing a stint as locum at Mt Isa Base Hospital. A mining town, Mt Isa is about nine hndred kilometres west of Townsville. The same sort of distance as Brisbane is to Sydney but nevertheless in the same local telephone book and same area health service.

The doctor servicing Doomadgee, a remote Aboriginal community, rang to arrange to send a pregnant woman to us. Apparently she had had something like six or seven children, I can't remember the exact number, all delivered by Caesarean section. Unfortunately, she had not looked after them so all of them had been removed from her care by Social Services. Not wanting to have this coming baby also taken away from her, she had kept her pregnancy secret and avoided all medical contact. They finally caught up with her, and the doctor rang me with that information and to tell me that, as near as they could tell, she was somewhere around term. She needed a Caesarean because a normal birth was not an option after so many previous Caesareans. Also, her baby was a breech – that is, coming bottom first.

I said no problem, send her along as soon as transport arrangements could be made and we would do the Caesarean. Transport was to be by the Royal Flying Doctor Service (RFDS) and it would fit in with the RFDS schedule to bring her the following morning.

The doctor rang me again that night to say that she was now bleeding. Obviously, she could not wait for a convenient time for transport and the RFDS was on its way as an emergency. A little later, I had a phone call from the RFDS doctor, who was equipped with a portable ultrasound machine. She told me that the ultrasound had shown the cause of the now heavy bleeding was a placenta praevia – that is, the placenta was lying in the lower part of the uterus and bled as the uterus started to contract and the lower segment started to be taken up as part of the normal process of the cervix opening for childbirth.

In theory, it would have been sensible to take the lady to the larger intensive care facilities for both mother and child at Townsville but it would take an extra couple of hours to get there and that delay was dangerous as the bleeding was now so heavy. I asked when they expected to arrive at Mt Isa and met them on arrival.

As, under these circumstances, an emergency hysterectomy was very much on the cards, I explained to the lady that this was the case and obtained consent, which I believe was genuine 'informed consent' as she was lucid enough to talk to sensibly. This was quite remarkable as the RFDS had a portable machine to measure haemoglobin, the red stuff in the blood that carries oxygen and their little machine, while not as accurate as a proper laboratory test, indicated that there was so little haemoglobin that it showed as zero on testing. In other words, she had already nearly bled out. Needless to say, we wasted no time getting her to the operating theatre.

When I opened her abdomen, instead of seeing the front of the uterus as one would expect, I was greeted by the placenta itself, which had ruptured through the previous Caesarean scar. I quickly pushed it aside and delivered the baby, which to everyone's relief had survived. Removal of the placenta was no problem but, as it had been in the lower segment of the uterus, which does not contract so well at this stage, the part where the placenta had been continued to bleed and the usual measures to control the bleeding had no effect.

Mostly when an emergency hysterectomy is necessary at Caesarean, it is done as a subtotal hysterectomy, where the upper part of the uterus only is removed. This is a much simpler operation and one which I had done several times in my career. However, on this occasion the bleeding was coming from the lower part of the uterus, so the more complex total operation had to be done, removing the entire uterus as it was the lower part that was bleeding.

Thankfully, that went quite uneventfully but we were still in trouble. Having bled so much, she had developed a condition known as 'consumption coagulopathy'. That is, she had used up all the clotting factors in her body, so her blood was unable to clot and she kept bleeding even though I had done all the stitching and so on that was required. However, pressure on an area of bleeding does control the bleeding. One hopes that after a period of prolonged firm pressure the bleeding will have stopped but not so this time.

We used up all the available materials at Mt Isa. Townsville had been contacted and my former colleague from there, Dr David Watson, was on his way with clotting factors to transfuse and hopefully stop the bleeding.

In the meantime, someone had called the general surgeon to come and help me. I can't remember his name but he was a very pleasant and thoroughly competent young man. He could add nothing to what I had so far done but it was as well he was there as, having to wait several hours for David to come from Townsville, we were stuck having to stand there and press on the packs we had placed on the bleeding areas. So the two of us took it in turns to stand and hold while the other had a break.

Eventually, David arrived with the goodies. They were duly transfused but the bleeding still did not stop, resuming as soon as the pressure on the bleeding area was relaxed. I controlled the situation by packing her abdomen with as many surgical sponges as I could fit in and closed the abdominal wall over them, thus maintaining pressure on the bleeding points. David took her and the baby back to Townsville and the packs were removed at another operation a couple of days later, by which time her clotting system had sorted itself out. Fortunately, both mother and baby did well. And of course, as she had had a hysterectomy, there was going to be no encore performance!

The Director of Medical Services at Mt Isa later told me that the hospital dealt with one or another form of emergency of this sort of gravity and urgency about once a month.

For the last year or two of my locum work, I worked almost exclusively at Wagga Wagga, which I enjoyed very much. Very congenial company; the department head was a colleague and friend whom I knew from when he had done a locum for us at Townsville and the other staff, medical and midwifery, being very congenial and easy to work with, and Wagga is a nice place.

Nevertheless, I was finding the work was tiring me more and more and decided it was time to pull the plug. Heather was now happy for me to do so from the financial aspect.

On Saturday 7 December 2013, I performed my last ever surgical operation and delivered my last baby. Concurrently. It was a Caesarean. I was on call for the hospital that weekend so came off duty at eight a.m.. Monday 9 December 2013. I stayed for the usual morning handover meeting then left. I was now officially unemployed again! I was seventy- one years, six months and four days old when I retired.

Usually, I flew to Wagga but on this occasion had chosen to drive. There is a fantastic aircraft museum at Temora, about an hour's drive north of Wagga that has Australia's only two flying Spitfires. I had arranged to sit in one of their Spitfires to celebrate.

After that, I drove as far as Andrew's place in western Sydney and stayed with them before proceeding home.

For some time, I had been having a lot of attacks of rapid heartbeat (atrial fibrillation, AF). I did not realise it but was on the wrong medication. I only just made it driving back home.

After that, I got worse and had no energy. I mean none. If I went downstairs to my workshop, just going down there took it out of me sufficiently that I couldn't do anything in the workshop but had to wait and gather up enough strength to come back upstairs. Yet my colleague who was prescribing the medications assured me all was well. I am sure I was getting all sorts of irregular heart rhythms as a consequence of inappropriate medication.

Heather was in Portland and I went down to visit her. I wasn't very well. I collapsed and lost consciousness in the street, much to the consternation of concerned passers-by.

The doctors at Portland were very good and sent me to the excellent cardiac unit at Geelong. Against my protests, I might add. I just wanted to go home. Instead, I had a ride in the back of an Air Ambulance King Air.

Associate Professor John Amarena and his team at Geelong were superb. They got me on the right medication. They could not find a reason for my collapse, so they would not let me home until they put in a defibrillating pacemaker. Fortunately, the defibrillator has not had to work. I'm pretty sure the problem was a side-effect of excessive wrong medication. The pacemaker part has kept my heart rate minimum sixty (better than in the forties!) and this has restored my energy to a reasonable level.

All that has meant that I no longer have a valid medical for my pilot's licence and I don't feel I have the energy to fight CASA over it. I'm happy with what I had and am enjoying putting my efforts into the models. Some of my modelling projects have been waiting twenty-five years, so I'm pleased to be attending to them at last.

They referred me for follow-up to Dr John Atherton's excellent cardiac unit at the Royal Brisbane and Women's Hospital. It has taken some time but my heart rhythm seems OK now and I am enjoying my time in the workshop, flying my models and doing a few things around the house.

We used accrued Qantas frequent flyer points to go to England and Europe in 2017. It was great seeing some friends. Andrew and his two younger children came, so it was a family affair. We went on to Budapest, where we babysat our American granddaughter Skye while her mum went to a music festival, and Andrew met us in Vienna and we all drove to the site of the slave labour camp at Viehofen, just north of St Polten. It's all parkland now and has been flooded as a recreational lake but there are memorials to the camp there.

We stayed in a rented apartment in Budapest for three weeks and I must say I really enjoyed being there. We caught up with my cousin Pisti and his wife Zsuzsi and also a colleague whom I had got to know when on study leave, and I visited the local model flying club.

And of course our youngest son, Michael, now calling himself Raphael, lives in Budapest, working in IT, so we had the rare and valuable opportunity of catching up with him also.

I didn't enjoy the trip back so much, though. I don't think I'll do such long-haul travel again, although Heather and I have done some cruises recently and find we enjoy those.

I know that when I get to Heaven I won't want to come back but all the same I hope I can have a bit longer pottering around in my retirement on this earth.

In case you're wondering no, I don't miss medicine at all. Been there, done that!

Part 3
My Spiritual Journey

Before We Start

I am a man of science, medical science anyway. I have held academic posts at both the University of Queensland and James Cook University. I have published articles in peer-reviewed journals. I have given presentations at international scientific meetings. I have given scientific talks to colleagues at international and national venues.

I have been chided by colleagues ('Peter!') when I have mentioned God in conversation. There are those who, conveniently forgetting that there are a lot of people of science who are Christians or otherwise are believers, feel that we don't need the concept of God as we have science to explain everything.

Science is the study of everything. Since when does knowing how something works indicate, let alone prove, that no one made it? Yet that's what they try to tell us. They differentiate a flint arrowhead from a piece of gravel as it is obvious someone must have designed and fashioned the arrowhead but they say that this incredibly complex human body just fortuitously made itself, 'evolved'.'

You would expect that if a God cared enough to make all this, He would leave some record of Himself. Many believe the Bible is legends and folklore and many base their judgement of the Bible on ignorance and misconceptions. Close scrutiny reveals that the Bible is very well documented indeed. I won't go further into that now.

'Religion' can mean different things. To me, it is my relationship with God and eminently logical. But for so many, religion is inextricably bound up with culture and this has a great influence on people's thinking. This concept underlies so much of the story of my own experience.

My faith is highly relevant to my memoirs as, quite frankly, had I not been aware of God's continuing presence with me throughout all the ups and downs, I could not have made it.

My Origins

I have already told how I come from a Jewish family.

My mother never spoke to me about these things but I have learnt that while in the camp she said Jesus visited her and told her that she would get through it all.

I remember when she sent us to Sunday school at St Paul's Church of England she explained that we were actually Presbyterian but she did not want us, us kids at any rate, to have to go across the busy Pacific Highway. St Paul's was just up the road from us.

I have no idea why she felt affiliated with the Presbyterian Church. I read somewhere that after she had had her vision of Christ she spoke with a Catholic priest who put her off by saying how it would take time and lessons before she could convert.

At any rate, we went to St Paul's, where I grew up in the Sunday School. We transferred to St Barnabas' Roseville East when we moved to East Roseville in 1955. At St Barnabas' I proceeded through Sunday school and in due course the Junior Fellowship.

The Sydney diocese of the Church of England/Anglican Church was, at least in those days and probably still, 'low church' and very evangelical in its teaching. Evangelical in this context means accepting the Bible as the Word of God, with the corollary of Jesus as being part of the Godhead, the Trinity, and accepting His atoning death on the cross for our sins as the culmination of the Jewish substitutionary sacrificial system.

I continued in this direction of Christian training and education in the Evangelical Union at university. I knew that I am ethnically Jewish but when my mother decided, she decided. I grew up knowing nothing of Jewish things. When my uncle Leo Taub in New York wrote 'Mazel Tov!' to me in response to the birth of our first son Ian, I had to look it up. I had even grown up on the very WASP North Shore of Sydney. Most of the Jewish population was in the eastern suburbs. I was completely 'gentilised'.

It was not until much later that I realised how deep one's Jewishness goes. In Sunday school we had Bible stories which included all the good

Old Testament (Jewish T'nach) stories. Right from the beginning, Adam and Eve, the fall, Noah and the flood, Joseph, Pharaoh, Moses, Joshua, Samson, Samuel, David and Goliath, the seventy-year exile, Daniel in the lions' den and so on.

I thought about all this. The Bible was the record of God's dealing with the human race. The Old Testament stories were about God's people the Jews. We were taught stories about 'the children of Israel'. In contrast, Jews spoke of Moses and so on not as 'the children of Israel' but as 'us'. Yet the church, and all the Christians I knew, were all gentiles. Had the church taken on the mantle of 'God's people'? These Old Testament stories segued seamlessly into the New Testament.

I didn't know it then but I realise now that we were being tacitly taught replacement theology. I don't think there was any anti-Jewish intent; I think it was simple naïve ignorance, perhaps coupled with Australian egalitarianism. Indeed, one of the characteristics of our church community was the kindness and acceptance shown us. We must have been Jewish if we were Holocaust survivors; we were certainly 'New Australians' struggling with the language and culture, yet these folk showed us nothing but true Christian love.

And so I went on, furthering my Christian education at university via the Evangelical Union (EU). This was no small thing as it was a major point of discussion in the anatomy dissecting room!

It is only of recent times that I have realised some of the drawbacks. The evangelical approach is highly oriented to correct doctrine. Doctrine is important. It is the facts. But we tended to forget that the purpose of having your facts right is to enable you to get your relationship to God right. Looking back on it, one could be forgiven for thinking that whatever we may have taught about 'salvation (entry to Heaven) by faith', we were really preaching entry to Heaven based on passing a doctrine exam. The reality is that you get there because your relationship with God has been restored.

So I grew up with the knowledge of God and have always had a consciousness of His presence. I am not very good at long prayer times but I know God is with me at all times and talk to Him without hesitation. I can assure you, God is very real and makes His presence felt.

One day as I was walking home from Roseville station after school with a couple of very active Christian friends, one of them asked me, 'Peter, are you a Christian?' to which I replied, 'I try to be.' He then explained that a Christian is one who accepts that Jesus' death on the cross atoned for our sins, so our sins no longer separated us from God. Having that explained to me, I answered without hesitation, 'Yes, then, I am.'

We stayed as active members of the Anglican Church until the church we were attending lost its direction and became spiritually dead. We went across to the local Pentecostal church, as the pastor there, Ian Woods, had shown interest and support in some of the things we were doing.

We never looked back. Ian and his wife Joan have remained friends, although Ian passed away rather young a couple of years ago. We now attend a very friendly and alive church in nearby Caboolture.

My Journey

My mother never liked her father-in-law, my paternal grandfather Fulop. I never realised why until the last few years.

My youngest son Michael, now Raphael ben Shmuel, had decided he was going to revert to his roots and embrace Judaism. He asked me what my Jewish or Hebrew name was. I didn't even know I had one. Having decided to be a Christian and no longer Jewish there was no way my mother was going to update me on that. Oy veh, never!

I happened to be in Budapest where the records are at the Great Synagogue. How they survived the war when the Nazis so badly trashed the place I have no idea. Anyway, I asked if I could check.

After some fiddling about getting there at a suitable time and so on, I went to the place they kept their records. There was a wall of bookshelves with large volumes like the books of labour ward records we used to keep. The rabbi asked me what year, so I told him. He asked me what date, so I told him when I had been born.

He got down the correct book for that year, opened it to the correct date, and there was my entry. Alas, it was written in Hebrew, not Hungarian. After a short delay, the young rabbi who could read Hebrew came along and translated it.

My Hebrew name is Shmuel ben Shrage Halevi.

The 'Halevi', Levite, obviously quite impressed the young rabbi.

So my son Michael is now Raphael ben Shmuel.

It was some time later, when I told my cousin Sylvia about this, that she told me her father's (my father's brother Tivi's) Jewish name, which was also ben Shrage. How can that be? 'Ben' is 'son of'. My uncle Tivi is son of his father Fulop, Hebrew name Shrage. So how can I, a generation down, be ben Shrage? I gather that my mother, having decided to be Christian, was not going to comply with any Jewish rituals on the eighth day. So Grandpa Fulop, when Mum wasn't looking, whisked me off to the synagogue. She never forgave him.

As not Dad but Grandpa had taken me, he made me his son. Poor Dad was disenfranchised and I am so sorry about that. It is easy to say he should have asserted himself, but World War II had not yet finished. If he had gone against Mum, World War III would have started. She was not to be crossed and the poor man was in a difficult position. You might say, 'no win'.

I have no idea what Dad's Hebrew name was. I never even knew there was such a thing, let alone that I had one, until decades after Dad's passing. Mum claimed not to know. I googled the synagogue at Banska Bystrica, where Dad's records would have been, but it had long gone.

How do I feel about this? At the time, many Jewish boys were not circumcised in an attempt to prevent the Nazis identifying them as Jewish and hopefully thus saving their lives. I guess it could have cost me my life. I am glad he did it. Being Jewish is my heritage.

I had a strange experience on our trip to England in 1969. The aircraft stopped to refuel in a couple of places en route from Hong Kong to Athens. One in Bombay (now Mumbai), India, and the other in Tel Aviv, Israel.

Heather stayed on board in Tel Aviv, maybe because she had just gotten Ian off to sleep. I got off to stretch my legs. As I walked from the plane to the transit lounge in the middle of the night, I had an irresistible urge to touch the soil of Israel. I looked everywhere for some soil. I mean soil, not concrete or vinyl floor. I desperately looked for a flower bed, a patch of lawn, anything, but could find none. An Israeli soldier, with rifle slung over his shoulder, told me to get in the building so I thought I had better not argue. I left disappointed that I had not been able to touch the soil of Israel.

This intense desire to touch the soil of Israel came as a total surprise

and the disappointment stayed with me for forty-one years until in October 2010 we went to Israel. I knelt down and kissed the ground.

I may not have given my Jewish identity a second thought beyond being aware of it, yet discovered that there is an incredible bond between Jews and their homeland.

I also became aware of another phenomenon. There were several Jewish boys in my year at school, and again at university. They were not close friends but I seemed to feel reasonably at one with them. I mean, folk with whom I felt some degree of affinity turned out to be Jewish.

On the other hand, there were several Hungarians in my year at university. While on cordial terms with them, somewhat to my surprise I did not feel the bond I thought there should have been. We were friendly enough, especially as we have got older and see each other at reunions, but I'm talking more than that.

In that time also, I have made several trips to Hungary, brushed up my language – well, a bit – and acquired a Hungarian passport (for ease of travel in the EU, although Britain has Brexited since). Yet I don't feel the same bond as I do with my Jewish colleagues. I think it's deep in the spirit.

God's Chosen People?

How are the Jews, the nation of Israel, God's chosen people?

I believe there are two aspects to that. One is that it is through the Jewish nation that the Messiah was to come, the One who would reconcile us with our Father. The other is that the Jews are used in the Bible as representative of the whole human race. As such, their behaviour illustrates every aspect, good and bad, of all humankind:

For example, on the one hand, the Hebrew people, as they came out of Egypt and became the nation of Israel, having experienced the miracles leading up to the exodus from Egypt, then the miracles of the exodus itself, had such a short memory that the moment Moses' back was turned when he went up to Mt Sinai, they immediately turned their backs on God and made and worshipped the golden calf.

But compare this to the behaviour of Caucasian Christian nations. When I was a child, everybody went to Sunday school and, whatever their later choices, everyone knew the basics. Yet in my own lifetime, within a few short decades, our society has totally rejected and forgotten our Judaeo/Christian heritage and few have any idea at all of the Bible, what's in it or what its message is.

And again, in an introduction to the short Old Testament/T'nach book written by the prophet Habbakkuk, as part of the NKJV Bible downloadable from the internet, it says, 'Habakkuk ministers during the death throes of the nation of Judah. Although repeatedly called to repentance, the nation stubbornly refuses to change her sinful ways. Habakkuk, knowing the hardheartedness of his countrymen, asks God how long this intolerable condition can continue. God replies that the Babylonians will be His chastening rod upon the nation...'

This book of prophecy was written in the mid to late seventh century BC, not long before the Babylonian siege and conquest of Jerusalem in 586 BC.

It does not take much imagination to apply this to the times in which we find ourselves living in Western society today.

Is our society intolerant? I have written a lot about anti-Semitism, yet look at the behaviour of some ultra-religious Jews who will physically prevent anyone even driving a car on the Sabbath. Are these people taking it too far? The Ten Commandments tell us not to work on the Sabbath. Most Jewish institutions will have a 'Sabbath lift' which automatically stops at every floor on Saturday so one does not need to do the 'work' of pushing the button. Or taking it further, there are those Jews who buy toilet paper in packets of sheets so they don't have to do the 'work' of tearing the sheets off the roll. (Presumably they tear the packets open before sundown Friday.)

If the Jews are examplars for the rest of humanity, it is to be expected that the examples are somewhat exaggerated in order to make the point. It may be that being a stickler for not 'working' on the Sabbath misses the point of the original intent of God's law, that we are made such as to need a break at intervals. But are there equivalents in modern society?

We need look no further than the law – that is, the laws of our land. The purpose of the rules of proper procedure in court and proper regulations for the handling of evidence and so on are there so justice can be done. Yet our judges and lawyers are so adept at applying these to the 'letter of the law' that the original purpose is defeated and these rules are manipulated regularly with the purpose of getting guilty parties off.

Yes indeed, being 'God's chosen people' is not a cause for pride but an onerous burden. It is not an excuse for racism, in either direction. We cannot control who we are born to be and the Bible tells us that God loves us all equally at an individual level.

Jewish or Christian, or Can You Be Both?

One of my Jewish colleagues, with whom I went to both school and university, asked me when we met a while back, whether I was Jewish or Christian. There are those who believe you can't be both and you can no longer be a Jew if you become a Christian.

That's actually a hard question to answer. There are problems on both sides. But should there be two sides?

There are several reasons why this is contentious, the most glaring one being the way people calling themselves Christians have treated Jews for a very long time. One need not elaborate too much on this. Anti-Semitism is found from way back.

Part of the reason is cultural. To me and other like-minded people, a Christian is someone whose relationship to God has been restored by the atoning sacrificial death of Christ. To many people, though, it is cultural, perhaps more so until the very recent past as the world is polarising so that our nations are no longer calling themselves Christian but secular with no state religion.

Until recently, to a Jew, every Caucasian gentile was a 'Christian'. This is a cultural perception. How can one expect a Jewish person to be open to the arguments for Jesus being the Jewish Messiah when people who are allegedly His followers perpetrate the most heinous acts of violence against Jews?

It's all very well to say one should look to Jesus, not to people who claim to be His followers but do not observe His teachings. But try telling that to someone like my late aunt by marriage, who tearfully told us of her father, a respected and loved member of his community who contributed more than his share, yet when anti-Semitic emotions ran rampant, said, 'They killed him.'

I challenge those evangelical Christians who believe that everyone who does not believe in Jesus, including those who have never even heard of Him, will go to Hell. Yes, it's true that 'there is no other name', and that 'No one comes to the Father but by me.'

It all too often gets forgotten that it is Jesus, not narrow-minded humans, who will be the judge. It is up to Him to adjudicate and decide who will get there. And it is as well not to forget that 'Man looks on the outward appearance but God looks on the heart.' (1 Samuel chapter 16 verse 7, Old Testament of the Bible or Jewish T'nach.)

Some Jewish leaders try to discredit Christianity by quoting the Shema, found in three places in the Torah, the Books of the Law in the Old Testament or T'nach, 'Behold O Israel, the Lord our God is one.' They accuse Christians of polytheism, worshipping three gods.

While the concept of the Trinity may be beyond our ability to understand, nevertheless God is one God, manifest in three persons. This is not the place to examine this further, but if Christians are excluded because they allegedly believe in not one but three Gods, then how come Jews who are atheists are still Jews? 'No God' is not 'one God'.

If one examines the scriptures closely, there are about three hundred Old Testament/T'nach prophecies which are fulfilled in the person of Christ. It has been worked out that the statistical odds of one person fulfilling even eight prophecies by chance is one in 100,000,000,000,000,000 and of one person fulfilling 48 prophecies is one in ten to the 157th power. Jesus Christ fulfils not eight, not forty-eight but three hundred.

That's all very well, but once again we must ask, what can one expect from Jewish people if for two thousand years people calling themselves Christians have persecuted them in the truly horrendous ways that are recorded in history?

Nevertheless, as Huxley said, 'Facts do not cease to exist because they are ignored,' no matter how good the justification to ignore them is.

As for gentile Christians who subscribe to 'replacement theology', sometimes referred to as 'spiritual Israel' (a term not found in the Bible to my knowledge), while they may claim to be Bible-believing they neglect so much of the apostle Paul's writings, especially the epistle to the Romans, around chapter 11.

It is forgotten that the New Testament was written by Jews for a largely Jewish readership. It is forgotten that Jesus is the Jewish Messiah. It is forgotten that it was the Romans, not the Jews, who actually killed Him. It is forgotten that Jesus died for the sins of the world, including both Jew and gentile. He laid down His life to save us; it was not forcibly taken from Him by either the Jews or the Romans of the day.

It is interesting to note that with the huge rise in anti-Semitism today there is a concurrent rise in persecution of Christians for their faith and that today Jews and true Christians are at last coming closer together. There are more and more Jews like myself who recognise Jesus as the Messiah and more and more Christians from the Bible-believing churches who stand shoulder to shoulder with the Jewish people, despite there still being too much anti-Israel, anti-Jewish sentiment among some Christians.

So where does that leave me? Have I changed my position?

I must admit that I am not as comfortable being called a 'Christian' as I used to be. I don't worry too much about it because it's often easier to keep it simple but in some ways I prefer to be called a 'Messianic Jew' or a 'completed Jew'.

I was not brought up in the Jewish way of life and am only now becoming aware of some of the traditional Jewish holidays, acknowledging and, whenever I can, observing them but not in an overly religious or obsessive way. The law has been superseded because it has been fulfilled. Nevertheless, those traditions are redolent with meaning.

A very pleasing aspect of today's world is that many Bible-believing churches are becoming increasingly conscious and supportive of Israel and all Jewish people and there is a greater friendship developing between gentile Christians and Jews.

I came into a world where there were those who were trying to eliminate all Jews, and true Christians in those lands who stood up against that were liable to suffer the same fate.

I am leaving to my grandchildren a world where there are those radicals who again want to kill all Jews, in Israel or elsewhere, a world in which persecution of people for their Christian faith is at unprecedented levels, a world in which people in our own society are losing their jobs, losing their academic freedoms, even going to jail, for standing by the principles in which they believe.

> *'Plus ça change, mais plus c'est la même chose.'*

Bakony Woods bandit. (Photo from web)

Kati Partos (née Weisz) with her children Hermin, Jeno, Yolan and Yanka (seated).

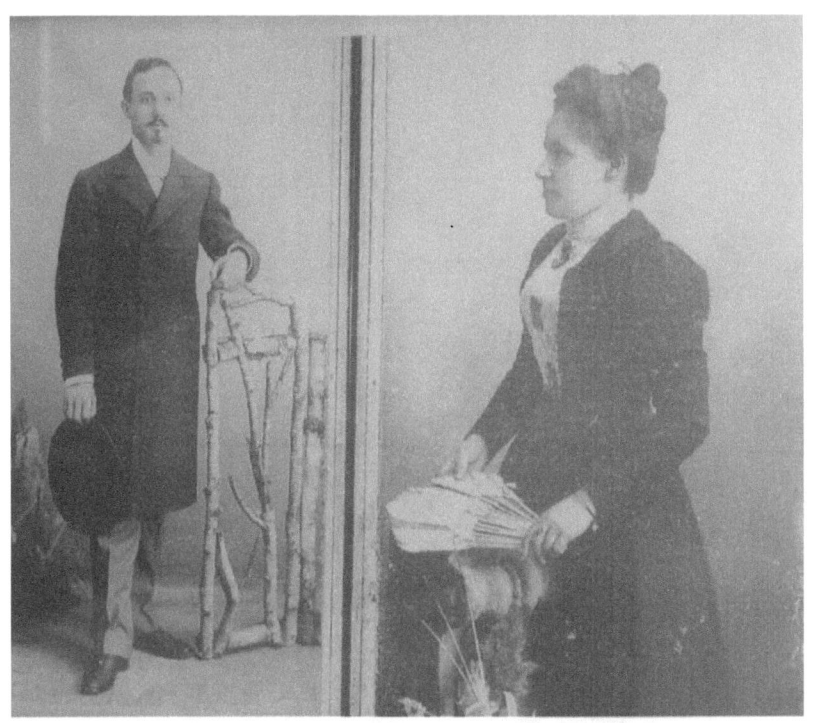

Founders of the American branch of the family: Moricz Taub and wife Mina (née Krausz), my great aunt.

Krausz family, c. 1922.
Back row: Lilli, Tivi, my father Imre, Nusi, Yolan, Karoly. Front row: Elli, Fulop.

With Sheila and Gilbert, Pittsburgh, 2009.

Fulop Krausz.

The Krausz boys: Tivi, Imre, Karoly.

My mother Clara and her older brothers, c. 1916.

Clara and Imre, 1935.

Pot that survived bombing.

The forced labour gang, early on. My father (left) and Joe Fisher (right) highlighted.

Mauthausen inmates pulling down German eagle after liberation. Little French hero in coat, far right.

The little French hero, Mr Choumoff, an inmate at the same time as my father, Mauthausen, April 2000.

*American hospital for liberated former concentration camp inmates.
My father was saved by one of these. (Photo from web)*

Aerial view of labour camp.

With Dr Balog's daughter Olga and grandson Miki Granski, Tel Aviv, October 2010.

Our father with Paul and me, 1946 (?).

Paul and me on the balcony at 7 Hernad utca, Budapest, c. 1947, with cousins John and Anne Elfer.

7 Hernad utca, showing the balcony.

Heather and me in the courtyard of 7 Hernad utca. Our old front door is above right.

Seeeing us off from Budapest, 14 August 1948. Back: my mother, Grandma Hermin, cousin John, Grandpa Fulop. Front: Paul, cousin Anne Elfer, me.

Petit Arc de Triomphe, Paris, 1948. Dad and me bottom right.

Margit Strauss and children with Grandma, Paul and me at Chatswood, 1952–53.

Lilly, John and Anne arrive, 1953.
Back: Mum, Lilly, Dad, John, Tivi. Front: me, Anne, cousin Sylvia Karas, Paul.

At Roseville, late 1960s. L to R: Mr & Mrs Elbert, Anne, Dad, Lilly, Mum, Jeno and Elizabeth Partos, Susan Fisher, Susan Karas.

With Paul and cousins Cathy Fisher (now Wills) and Sylvia (now Deutsch OAM).

Paul and me at 16 Tessa Street, Chatswood, c. 1952–53.

Infants school, 1950. Roger and me circled.

With Roger, San Francisco, 2008.

Brochure for Dad's product Ferropro, Australia's first corrosion treatment.

Semper Seal Chemical's offices and factory, Lane Cove. Tivi was the architect.

Mum and Dad, c. 1959. Photo taken, developed and printed by me.

Singer 9.

*Student group at RNSH with tutor Chook Fowler.
Taken with self-timer, developed and printed by me.*

Wheelchair basketball.

Heather's dad, Dreadnought boy, aged 15.

Medical staff, Swindon Maternity, 1970. Abdul and me circled; Jones, Yates and Jolly in front; ABC obscured.

Gordon Jolly, 2006.

With Vyv and Joan Jones, and Michael Yates, 2006.

Heather, Ian and MG 1100, UK,

With Susan Karas when she and Tivi visited us in the 'bungalow', Swindon, late 1970.

Little had changed when we revisited Harlow in 2006. I walked to work here from our flat. Maternity building on right.

Revisiting our Harlow accommodation.

Me and our three boys, Albury, 1975.

The boys and me with Treble, c. 1976.

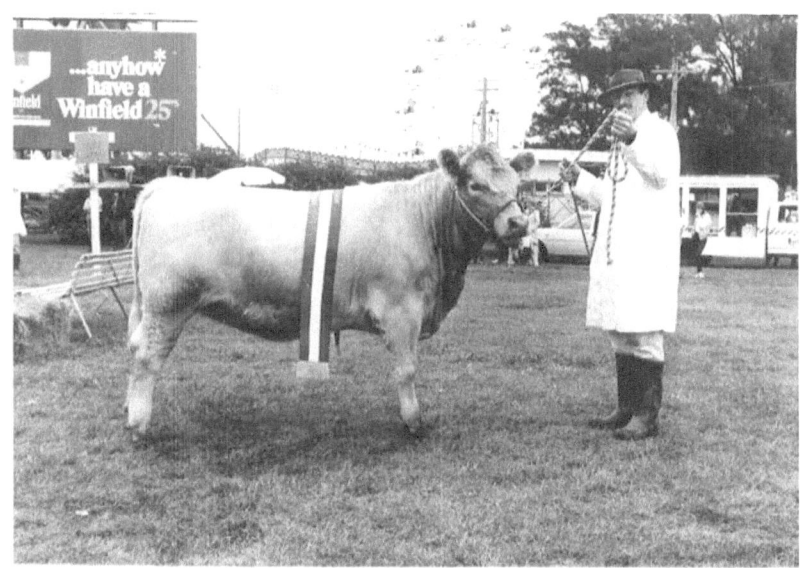

Our finest Murray Grey achievement – champion heifer at Hawkesbury Show.

With Eric Green at my farewell afternoon tea, Townsville, January 2008.

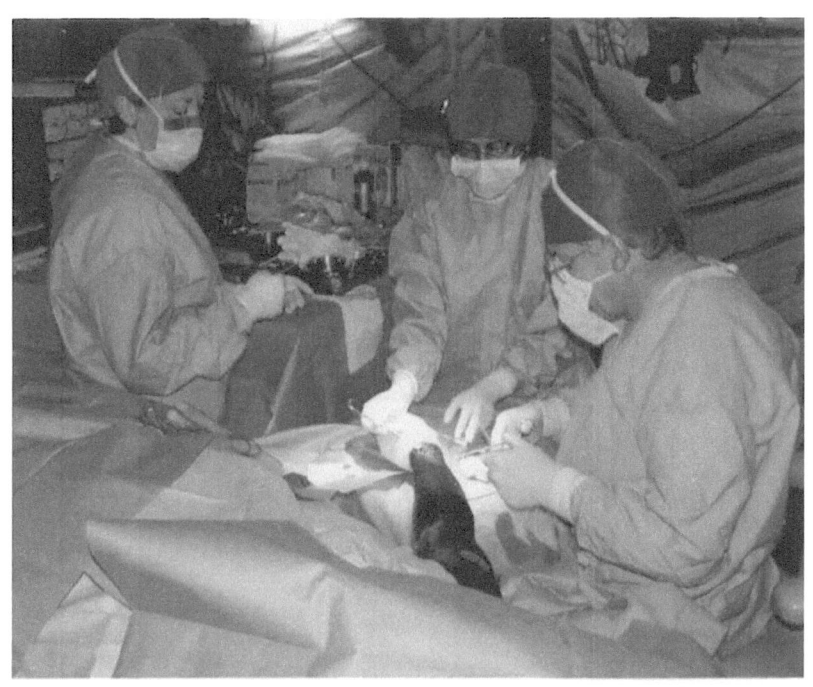

Patching up a machete fight combatant, Bougainville, 1999.

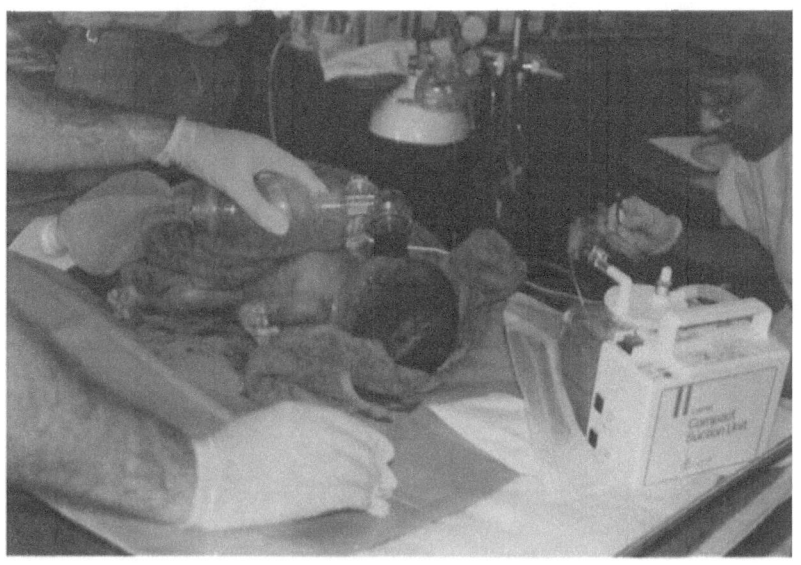

Baby just delivered by Caesarean section, Bougainville, 1999.

Appendix

Family members known to have perished in the Holocaust:

Frida (née Krausz)
Frida's husband
Jeno Elbert's first wife
Jeno Elbert's child(ren)
Mrs Elbert's first husband
Katherine Krausz Springer
Katherine Springer's husband
Karoly Krausz
Yanka Partos Eisler
Zsigmond Eisler
Andor Elfer
Susan Kardos Karas's first husband

Acknowledgements

My heartfelt thanks go to the following people without whom I could not have written this memoir.

First to my wife Heather, who has been a true soulmate who has stuck with me and encouraged me through thick and thin, who has shared my joys and sorrows and given me three great sons.

Also to those three sons who have borne with me when, due to the nature of my work, I was called away or too exhausted to give them the attention they deserved. I have only recently come to realise the effect of their father being a child survivor has had on them.

Then to those who were such good role models for me in my formative years: Sunday school teachers, Junior Fellowship leaders, school teachers and others.

To the late Rev, Dr Robert Schuller, whose Hour of Power ministry from the Crystal Cathedral in LA, sustained us when we were in a very down time and also the late Pastor Ian Woods and his wife Joan for the same and for his friendship until his untimely passing.

I hope that this memoir achieves its aim in part to be a tribute to those who taught me in my medical training years. They are in the appropriate part of the narrative.

To my aunt Susan Fisher, whose information and insights into the family were invaluable; my cousin Sylvia Deutsch OAM (née Karas), for her sharing of so much family history; and my cousin Cathy Wills (née Fisher), for the photograph of the forced labour gang with both our fathers in it.

To the late Stephen Matthews, founder of Ginninderra Press, and to Debbie Lee for working with me to publish this revised edition.

Last and most importantly, to the Lord God who saved me from the horrors of the Holocaust, who brought us to Australia, who strengthened me in all the trials and has provided all my needs and more.

www.ingramcontent.com/pod-product-compliance
Lightning Source LLC
Chambersburg PA
CBHW020524080526
44583CB00013B/724